Advanced Reviews for *Primer on Posttraumatic Growth: An Introduction and Guide*

Mary Beth Werdel and Robert Wicks provide a solid introduction to the field of post-traumatic growth. Their primer will be invaluable to students new to the field as well as those who work closely with survivors of trauma. Their Primer is packed with the latest research findings, positive psychology applications, and richly illustrated with clinical cases and examples from philosophy. Engaging and informative this book will help counselors to nurture the seeds of growth in their clients by becoming more mindful of the process of post-trauma change. A book full of wisdom and compassion.

Stephen Joseph, Ph.D.
Professor, Center for Trauma, Resiliency and Growth
University of Nottingham, UK
Author, *What Doesn't Kill Us: The New Psychology of Posttraumatic Growth*

How eye-opening to read this fascinating analysis of posttraumatic growth and to realize that, as a nurse/nurse educator, I have witnessed patients, families, students and colleagues struggling to find meaning in a loss, trauma, or significant change without fully considering the value of the trauma as setting the stage for growth.

The authors share meaningful anecdotes throughout each chapter as well as clinical cornerstones at the end of each chapter which summarize the discussion and provide the clinician with thoughtful recommendations to incorporate into practice . . .

This book is a gift not only to clinicians but to those dealing with posttraumatic stress, their families and friends. I am most appreciative of the opportunity to have it in my library.

Anne E. Belcher, PhD, RN, AOCN, ANEF, FAAN
Associate Professor and Director, Office for Teaching Excellence
The Johns Hopkins University School of Nursing

In the book *Primer on Posttraumatic Growth*, Mary Beth Werdel and Robert Wicks offer a sophisticated and multi-factorial introduction of possible positive adaptations after traumatization. They are sensitive to the delicate balance that exists between decline and growth and introduce a spectrum of responses that can develop over time in a subjective and non-linear fashion. For many, after the devastation of trauma comes the opportunity to rework a number of life dimensions. This book is an important and integrative addition to the literature on posttraumatic growth.

Christine A. Courtois, PhD, ABPP
Psychologist, Private Practice
Courtois & Associates, Washington, DC
Author, *Healing the Incest Wound: Adult Survivors in Therapy (Revised Edition)*
Recollections of Sexual Abuse: Treatment Principles and Guidelines
Co-Author (with Julian Ford), *Treating Complex Trauma Stress Disorder.*

Primer on
Posttraumatic Growth

An Introduction and Guide

Mary Beth Werdel & Robert J. Wicks

JOHN WILEY & SONS, INC.

LIBRARY OF CONGRESS CATALOGING-IN-PUBLICATION DATA:

Werdel, Mary Beth.
  Primer on posttraumatic growth : an introduction and guide / Mary Beth Werdel, Robert J. Wicks.
    p. cm.
  Includes bibliographical references and index.
  ISBN 978-1-118-10678-5 (pbk.)
  ISBN 978-1-118-22406-9 (ebk.)
  ISBN 978-1-118-23337-5 (ebk.)
  ISBN 978-1-118-26228-3 (ebk.)
  1. Emotions. 2. Distress (Psychology) I. Wicks, Robert J. II. Title.
  BF531.W44 2012
  155.2′4—dc23

                                                    2012015369

Mary Beth Werdel
In memory of
my brother, Thomas John Nazzaro; and
my role model, Crescentia Healy True

Robert J. Wicks
In memory of
Kelly Murray and her daughter, Sloane,
and
in honor of
her husband, Sean,
and
their daughters,
Jillian, Meghan, Maeve, Quinn, and Kieran

Kelly and her daughter, Sloane, died when a tree limb crushed part of their car during a terrible storm. Kelly was only 40 years old at the time, and Sloane was only 7. Kelly was a fine psychologist, passionate professor, gifted author, supermom, and loving wife. As her mentor and friend, I shall not only remember her in all those ways but also as the younger sister I never had.

The passion and resilience she had she shared with her husband, Sean, with Sloane, who died with her, and with her other children Jillian, Meghan, Maeve, Quinn, and Kieran, who live on. Since her death, Sean and Kelly's children have modeled what posttraumatic growth looks like in the flesh. Though they have never stopped loving Kelly, they have looked this tragedy in the eye and come out on the other side, developing talents and having insights that might never have been possible if this terrible event had never happened. They would trade it all I am sure to have her back, but because they cannot they have moved on in ways that inspire us all. Thank you. I am grateful to you all, and to you as well as Kelly and little Sloane I gratefully dedicate this book.

.

CONTENTS

ACKNOWLEDGMENTS

Every book has at least several heroes who come to the aid of a project and make it better. This *Primer on Posttraumatic Growth: An Introduction and Guide* is certainly no exception. We wish to thank Tina Buck for her editorial and research assistance. She repeatedly carefully reviewed the material to see if content and readability lived in the same manuscript.

Patricia "Tisha" Rossi, Executive Editor of John Wiley & Sons, had the enthusiasm and encouragement needed to help the co-authors transform an idea into a manuscript. Her involvement in this project made a difference, and the authors are deeply grateful to her for her presence and desire for excellence in a clinical area that is so important to so many people who have experienced serious trauma, yet hold out hope that something wonderful will still come of it, today.

INTRODUCTION

Many people, for much of their lives, are guided by a set of basic assumptions: The world is safe; bad things do not happen to good people; young people are not supposed to die. However, extremely stressful and traumatic life events can violate and even shatter these basic assumptions, resulting in experiences of distress as well as a sense of loss of control, meaning, and predictability. Renowned trauma expert Bessel van der Kolk (2006) described the experience of a traumatic event as one that may leave individuals feeling as if they have "lost their way in the world" (p. 278). This metaphorical language by van der Kolk highlights the close relationship between trauma and loss that is noted throughout the traditional psychological literature.

Even though trauma and extreme stress are arguably somewhat rare, everyone experiences internally framed negative events that have the capacity to challenge basic life assumptions in various forms at different times: rejection, illness, caring for an aging parent, unwanted dramatic changes at work, and divorce. More startling events such as rape, abuse, war, or physical attack can cause people to have a complete shutdown. Stressful events such as these, and the physical and psychological pain that may accompany them, are certainly an undesirable part of life.

Current psychological research highlights that even with full acknowledgment of the undesirability of negative life events, the process of enduring and learning from distress can offer a reward that has never before been encountered. This experience may provide new purpose or appreciation for life, creative coping skills, or improved relationships with self and others. The French existentialist philosopher Albert Camus (1968) wrote, "In the depths of winter, I finally learned that within me lay an invincible summer." Camus' words provide a clinical metaphor to compliment the one quoted earlier by van der Kolk. Sometimes, only once one finds the self in the depths of a significant stressful life event (that they did not cause but, like the seasons, by merely existing, are asked to encounter) can one ever come to discover within oneself this new source of light (perspective and meaning).

A benefit of this new sense of perspective and meaning has been both hinted at and boldly claimed by seekers and searchers in life. Yet, now as an outgrowth of the positive psychology movement, research demonstrates in greater detail—after numerous quantitative and qualitative studies—that how we respond to distress depends on several personal and environmental factors, some out of, but many within, our locus of control. In a moment of self-reflection (often after further guidance that is informal or formal, such as therapy or counseling), we can ask ourselves, do the factors that are within our control ultimately lead us to respond in ways that may deepen and make us more compassionate with ourselves and others or lead us only to numbness and bitterness?

These movements in the behavioral sciences in the field of positive psychology help inform us about the myriad ways that people can and do respond to stress and trauma. With a full awareness of the significant negative impacts of such events, the field of positive psychology has taken an interest in the positive benefits that people may come to experience as a result of enduring and learning from a traumatic or stressful life event. Although several terms exist to describe similar constructs, *posttraumatic growth*, a term coined by Tedeschi and Calhoun (1996), is perhaps the predominant term used now in the psychological literature to describe such positive life changes. Posttraumatic growth conceptually falls into one of three categories: changes in the *perception of self*, changes in *relating to others*, and philosophical changes of *priorities, appreciations, and spirituality* (Calhoun & Tedeschi, 2006).

Research on the process of posttraumatic growth states that the path to growth starts with people's pretrauma cognitive schema about the world and themselves. If they experience a stressful event that conflicts with their personal previously held assumptions about the world and themselves, distress is experienced. When this occurs, they then engage in both an automatic and deliberate rumination process about the stressful event and their responses to the event. Rumination ceases only when they are able to revise their old schema and/or adopt a new one. Changes in schema can include new understandings of the self, new values placed on relationships, or a different purpose in life (Calhoun & Tedeschi, 2006). The implication is that the loss associated with trauma need not represent the *full* trauma narrative. As a matter of fact, for some people, along with loss, and through enduring and learning from the loss, there is a sense of positive discovery. In addition, the process that can enhance such desirable results is informed and formed by such factors as social relationships, personality characteristics of the individual, the intensity of the stress, and even the relationship some people have with their understanding of the divine.

In the following example, Emily, a high school senior, reflects on how she responded to her mother's diagnosis of breast cancer in December 2001 and their journey together. Emily's mother had her first mastectomy that year when Emily was in fifth grade and her second in 2002. Emily writes about how she met the stress and trauma and its impact on her, her mother, and her younger sister:

> I took care of my mother after her chemo treatments, which left her completely drained and exhausted. I also made my sister smile, when reality was becoming too clear for her. With every treatment I grew up a little bit, accepting the level of maturity that was asked of me. Cancer made me grow up a lot quicker then I would have without it in my life. It made me take on responsibility. Most importantly it brought awareness and even hope into my life. . . . After completing the treatments with flying colors, my mom participated in a 3-day walk for breast cancer sponsored by Avon. I stood on the sidelines gazing up with pride at my mother, thinking, "She is the strongest and bravest person I know. She beat breast cancer."

Not only did Emily's mother survive her double mastectomy, but in 2004 she started a nonprofit program designed for children ages 10 to 18 whose loved ones suffer from cancer and other life-threatening illnesses. In Emily's words, "It's a program designed for kids to have fun and to know that they are not alone."

However, when Emily entered her freshman year of high school, her mother's cancer returned. So did Emily's stress and trauma, and so did Emily's growth.

> The cancer was back, and it was far more severe this time. It was spreading. My mom being the optimistic and determined woman that I loved decided to look into trial drugs. She went through months of tests and treatments. I stood by her side every step of the way.
>
> When I was 14-years-old, my mother's cancer had spread to her stomach and bones. By January of 2006 I knew that

my mother would most likely only be with me for another two years. In February I was given a rude awakening when my mother sat me down and told me those years had turned into a few months. Life became more real, and each day became more precious.

On March 12th those months turned into weeks. The next morning my sister and I were woken up by our aunts who told us that we were going to play hooky from school. Later that day, upon our arrival home, my sister and I were hit with the final blow. My mother was dying.

The next day, March 14th, 2006, my mother passed away. I grew up that day. I learned to take advantage of each day, and never take anything for granted, because life is more valuable then gold. You only have one life to live. My mother took advantage of hers; even with her cancer she made a difference in this world. I can only hope that one day I will do the same. Thank you, cancer.

Emily thanked cancer. As a 17-year-old, she grasped that the very disease that took the most precious person in her life, her base of emotional and physical security, was in some way presenting her with an opportunity to come to understand something about life for which she was quite grateful. At first glance, she seems to be either in denial or someone tremendous. But Emily's story, while individual, is neither merely anecdotal nor unique. There is strong data to support the psychological phenomena that what Emily described is also experienced every day by others who are psychologically traversing their own journeys with stress and trauma.

However, even though clinicians in the field and those who support clients (friends, family, coworkers, clergy) may be somewhat aware of the phenomena of posttraumatic growth, they may not be aware of the terminology, the abundance of research on the subject, and perhaps most importantly, the significant clinical implications of the research. Given this deficit, *Primer on Posttraumatic Growth: An Introduction and Guide* seeks to mine the empirical and theoretical material on posttraumatic growth and relate the two in order to provide insight, depth, and applications for both the clinicians who work with those who have experienced dramatic negative events in their lives and for the other people who support victims of trauma and extreme stress. This book will link the latest research in the area of posttraumatic growth with accessible clinical insights that will stress how a certain degree of mindfulness on the part of the counselor/therapist/cojourneyer can significantly contribute to a fuller, more accurate, clinical case conceptualization and thus to more successful clinical interventions relative to stress, trauma, and growth that are more efficacious.

Throughout, this primer will stress that clinicians and counselor educators need to be aware that there is an important balance when working with people who have experienced traumatic and extremely stressful life experiences. If clinicians expect certain growth on the part of the clients too quickly, then the clients may begin to feel guilty or shameful that they are not living up to the therapist's or others' understanding of what they ought to be discovering as survivors of trauma or stress. Clinicians and caregivers coming from such a vantage point would represent a great misreading of the literature on posttraumatic growth and would consequently have significant negative impacts on therapy or the informal helping relationship. On the other hand, if clinicians and caregivers operate without an awareness of the growth that can follow trauma, then they may miss the possibility to explore a real, and perhaps healing, place within the client's new schema. Clinically, the goal is the middle path: openness and awareness to the process of growth in clients, with no preconceived expectations or need for clients to undergo the experience.

The aim of this book is to lead clinicians and those in the clients' interpersonal circle who are available to support them into a deeper understanding of reality. If we remain curious, open, and mindful of positive possibilities, clients in the midst of their personal winters may slowly begin to exhibit in external ways the recognition of a newly discovered internal invincible summer. The orientation guiding this book is that in the case of trauma, extreme stresses, or major losses, the clinician's primary role is to be aware of the major elements of posttraumatic growth so, should they appear, the clinician is then prepared to nurture them in ways that welcome their taking root and growing during therapy when clinically appropriate.

In *Primer on Posttraumatic Growth: An Introduction and Guide*, the approach to each topic is fairly uniform. A succinct coverage of the topic is offered so access to the current thinking and research can be quickly reviewed. Each chapter concludes with three helpful sections. *First*, a quote from the research literature is presented so that clinicians may orient themselves and continue to fathom the ways the material may resonate with their work. *Second*, the clinical implications presented in each chapter are outlined at the conclusion of each chapter in order to allow readers to readily appreciate clinically relevant material. *Finally*, each chapter ends with a short suggested reading list for those who wish to take a deeper look at primary sources on the topic at hand.

To accomplish this overview, nine topics have been chosen as a way for the clinician, and those available to informally support the client, to become familiar with some of the central material on posttraumatic growth. **Chapter 1,** *Posttraumatic Growth: Concise History, Definitions, and Implications*, begins this process by presenting an *historical context for the concept of posttraumatic growth*, providing a timeline for work done thus far in the psychological field, as well as clarifying the up-to-date research on the theory of how growth occurs and the psychological factors that growth associates with the research literature. It points to various studies in the empirical research that document that posttraumatic growth may be experienced by persons undergoing such diverse trauma and the extreme stress that is part and parcel of HIV/AIDS diagnosis, cancer, bereavement, domestic violence, physical illness, brain injury, or experiencing 9/11-type terrorist attacks.

The authors then read across the studies to broaden consideration of the essential question: Who may experience growth from struggle? In addition, this chapter considers growth, which in the past has sometimes been erroneously viewed as being only a form of resistance or denial, as a possible profound beneficial cognitive shift in the making. This viewpoint is shown to be important for therapists to appreciate, because their vantage point can and does affect how they intervene and will in turn influence the outcomes of therapy.

Chapter 2, *Posttraumatic Growth: Truth or Myth?*, presents some of the main voices in the controversy surrounding posttraumatic growth that centers on the argument of *whether* the subjective experience of posttraumatic growth is a reality or an illusion (Sumalla, Ochoa, & Blanco, 2009). The argument exists partly because obtaining pretrauma scores of growth is, practically speaking, quite difficult (Ransom, Sheldon, & Jacobsen, 2008). Therefore, the chapter discusses a belief by some in the field that posttraumatic growth is not actual but perceived. It has been proposed that the experience of trauma drops an individual's level of functioning to a decreased level following the occurrence and that the growth a trauma victim reports is actually only a return to baseline functioning. Two theories that support this view of growth as being illusionary are reviewed: They are the temporal comparison theory (Albert, 1977) and the cognitive adaption theory (Taylor, 1983). The chapter then concludes with what researchers consider a less extreme response to the argument against growth—Maercker and Zoellner's (2004) Janus face model of self-perceived posttraumatic growth. From the vantage point of this model, posttraumatic growth is considered as having two sides—one representing veridical growth and the other illusion. The chapter closes with a discussion concerning the clinical implications of assessing the veracity of growth.

Chapter 3, *Meaning,* presents the important connections between meaning and growth, beginning with a discussion of ways one might understand meaning from a psychological framework. The chapter also introduces meaning as a distinctly human phenomenon (Baumeister & Vohs, 2002), serving as a basic human motivation (Frankl, 1969) that allows people to predict and control their personal and social environments, assists in both behavioral and affect self-regulation, and helps in fulfilling the need for purpose, value, self-efficacy, and self-worth (Baumeister, 1991).

Research psychologist Crystal Park's (2005a) Meaning-Making Model Paradigm for understanding stress and growth is highlighted here in an accessible level of detail for nonresearchers (with sources at the chapter's end for those who seek a broader treatment of the topic). We then explore the clinical tension that exists between the theoretical and empirical research, which suggests that the process of meaning-making is a central concern after stress and trauma. We also address the current belief that among the groups of people at the highest risk of not finding meaning are those who experience loss under traumatic circumstance (Davis, Wortman, Lehman, & Silver, 2000). Finally, several major productive therapeutic approaches to helping clients to successfully engage in the meaning-making process are provided. Consequently, this is an especially important chapter for clinicians who wish to be appropriately sensitive and in a better position to respond to trauma clients who are at a turning point in the therapy and are in an ideal position to consolidate recent gains in treatment so they can progress in finding a more adaptable view of themselves and the world.

In **Chapter 4,** *Cognitive Processing,* we explore the impact of cognitive processing on posttraumatic growth. Stress and trauma can destroy the cognitive assumptions that people hold about this world. Yet for psychological and emotional health, we need such organizational guides intact, making reconstruction of basic cognitive assumptions a necessity (Tedeschi & Calhoun, 2004). A lack of an organizational guide leaves one with distressing feelings, lack of comprehensibility, and lack of meaning. Together, such experiences are thought to set a person on a course of thinking about the event (or *ruminating* in Calhoun and Tedeschi's conceptualization) in either or both automatic and deliberate ways. For some, the rumination process will eventually lead to posttraumatic growth (Tedeschi & Calhoun, 2004). The timing of processing (directly after the event versus after some time has passed) and the content of ruminations (positive versus negative) are both explored. The chapter concludes with the role that clinicians may play in encouraging the processing of stressful and traumatic events in such a way that encourages psychological health and does not discourage growth.

Chapter 5, *Positive Emotions and Growth*, presents the *relationship between positive emotion and posttraumatic growth.* The approach is to first define *positive affect* and then to present the empirical studies that suggest an association between it and growth (Linley & Joseph, 2004). Of specific discussion in the chapter is a meta-analysis of 87 studies from 77 articles (Helgeson, Reynolds, & Tomich, 2006) that consistently points to the relationship. Later in the chapter the studies that provide conflicting information are offered and used as a basis to argue that the connection between growth and positive affect may necessitate a period of several years of treatment to become evident (Salsman, Segerstrom, Brechting, Carlson, & Andrykowski, 2009; Schaefer & Moos, 1998).

By way of concluding the coverage of this topic, an essential implication of the research that clinicians need be aware of in the treatment of trauma victims is highlighted: namely, to take care *not* to look for or expect growth too soon because of the danger this brings with it. By inordinately pushing for growth in the early stages of trauma and stress work, or by seeking to force the client into a seemingly ideal therapeutic position before the timing becomes possible, we run the risk of causing more suffering—all in the name of therapeutic progress! Though this therapeutic error may seem self-evident, unfortunately it is not, especially in the case of those clinicians who are aware of the promise of the literature on posttraumatic growth without possessing a full appreciation of the pacing and timing involved in achieving this very promise with those clients with whom it becomes possible.

Chapter 6, *Personality and Personal Attributes*, presents the relationship between posttraumatic growth and the personality facet of openness. The chapter begins with a very brief overview of the Five Factor Model of personality, which suggests that personality consists of the factors of neuroticism, extraversion, openness, agreeableness, and conscientiousness. Personality plays an important role in both how and why individuals experience any and all positive emotions. Personality not only colors the way each person perceives life events but also works to eventually return the person to pretrauma levels of subjective well-being following the traumatic experience (DeNeve & Cooper, 1998). The implication is that the very same event may be perceived as either more positive or more negative based on an individual's personality (Magnus, Diener, Fujita, & Pavot, 1993). Therefore, a person's posttrauma level of function and growth may be related to personality characteristics present both pre- and posttrauma. The chapter concludes with clinical applications of exercises for both clients and clinicians.

Chapter 7, *Relationships*, addresses the association between the human drive to be in positive and important interpersonal relationships (Baumeister & Leary, 1995); the dependency that humans have on their relationships with other human beings for meaning, affirmation, protection, and connection (van der Kolk, 2006); and how such views on relationships relate to posttraumatic growth experiences. Special emphasis is on how research on the relationship between social support and psychological flourishing suggests the importance of not merely the presence of positive social support in the process of posttraumatic growth but the absence of negative social support. The understanding of the importance of relationships relative to growth is placed within a cultural context.

In **Chapter 8,** *Forgiveness,* is portrayed as an action that can be extended toward all areas of posttraumatic growth: the self, another, and even, as was previously alluded to when the client sees it as essential, the divine image. The empirical research on the relationship between forgiveness and posttraumatic growth in the psychological literature is quite limited and relatively recent. Yet, even though the relationship between forgiveness and growth remains more or less admittedly an intuitive truth at this point in history (Fischer, 2006), available research is presented. The clinical implications of these exploratory studies and suggestions for future directions in research are examined by way of concluding this relevant area.

Chapter 9, *Faith, Suffering, and Religious Coping,* presents the connection between posttraumatic growth and religious and spiritual variables, both theologically and empirically. Starting with the theological foundation of the psychological process of posttraumatic growth, Christianity is highlighted as but one example of a major faith tradition. Included is the paradoxical nature of the Christian view of human suffering, which may lead to the development of character virtues (Roberts, 2007). The chapter then turns to the examination of religious and spiritual variables within a psychological framework. Empirical studies suggesting how religion and spirituality are both particularly useful are presented. After considering such positive associations between spirituality/religion and growth, the detrimental role that spiritual struggle can also possibly play in a person's experience of posttraumatic growth is addressed. Following this, the clinical implications of working with religious and spiritual themes with clients are explored, because this area is especially important for those professionals working with religiously committed clients.

Finally, the book concludes with a forward-looking chapter, *On the Road to Wisdom: Being a Mindful Companion on the Path to Posttraumatic Growth*: *An Epilogue,* which focuses particularly on the topic of wisdom and posttraumatic growth. The authors support the thinking of many of the authors in the field, which suggest the connection of growth and wisdom (Calhoun & Tedeschi, 2006). Taking the major studies on the area of posttraumatic growth as a whole, the theoretical arguments and empirical findings are in line with the idea that posttraumatic growth is in essence the acquisition of new wisdom. To be wise is a concept that is often associated with age and length of experience; however, trauma and stress have the potential of helping persons to grow wise beyond their chronological years. This brief epilogue also reflects on theoretical and empirical understandings of growth and significant aspects of the classical wisdom literature, providing a framework of hope for individuals and societies as we move ahead in an increasingly stressful and traumatized world.

Mary Beth Werdel
Fordham University
Robert J. Wicks
Loyola University Maryland

CHAPTER 1

POSTTRAUMATIC GROWTH: CONCISE HISTORY, DEFINITIONS, AND IMPLICATIONS

Kelly was a successful practicing psychologist who had recently been awarded tenure at her university. She was chair of a certificate program on trauma, a subject for which she received national attention as a result of her work after the September 11, 2001, terrorist attacks in New York, Washington, D.C., and Pennsylvania. Her book on personality disorders had just been published. For her intellect and achievement, she was respected and admired by her colleagues, many of whom over the years had come to call her a friend. And this was merely some of the good in her professional life.

She was also the mother of six children ages 12 years to 10 months. All girls. All beautiful girls. She was the wife of, and best friend to, her husband for 16 years. She was an active member of her children's schools, her church, and her community. She coached soccer. She mentored young girls. She actively lived the healthy life that she preached, jogging regularly, even training for a marathon. She seemed to find a way to touch the lives of the people with whom she interacted with a combination of humor, wit, and grace. In a word, she was *special.*

Of course, as many of us recognize from both our professional and personal lives, the degree to which we love and are loved does not protect us from stress or trauma. This certainly was true for Kelly and her family.

On a late June afternoon, while at a swim practice with four of her children, the skies started to darken, signaling that a tremendous thunderstorm was moving quickly into the suburb. With obvious concerns for her children's well-being, Kelly packed her children and two of their friends into her minivan to head home. They lived a mere 2.5 miles from the pool. As they made their way home, the winds intensified. The storm was later described as one of the most violent cells of thunderstorms that had been seen in that part of the country in a long while. The wind gusts were estimated to have exceeded 50 miles per hour, which apparently was strong enough to cause a giant branch from a 44-inch-wide red oak tree and the surrounding electrical wires to come crashing down on Kelly's minivan, instantly killing her and one of her children, and trapping one girl alive in the van on top of her dead friend waiting to be rescued. Witnessing the scene, a number of good Samaritans pulled all of the children out of the car, except for one daughter and her trapped friend. It was a terribly horrific scene.

As is the case with many stressful events, just as quickly as the darkness moved in, it lifted from the sky. When word started to spread about the death of such a loved woman and her daughter, that darkness began to pour into the hearts and minds of the people in Kelly's community as they were faced with the reality of such tragic, seemingly incomprehensible deaths of such a special mother, colleague, mentor, and friend, and of such a bright, promising 7-year-old girl.

At the funeral, Kelly and her daughter were laid to rest in the same coffin, her daughter positioned by a funeral home worker on her mother's chest, just as she had been placed 7 years before by a physician after her birth. That Kelly and her daughter died together for some made the death more than doubly tragic. The death of Kelly and her daughter brought more than 3,000 people to the funeral, each one to a different degree carrying their "why" question. Why Kelly? And why her daughter? Why together? Why at that millisecond? Why on that road? Why in that way? Why now?

Why Suffering?

As clinicians we often hear the questions associated with people's suffering. Tragedy is painfully part of the human experience. If we can find any people in our lives who can serve as examples of those who have not experienced any profound stress or trauma (if any do exist), such people are indeed the outliers—for now. We all come to learn that suffering is part of our narrative as people. Some of us who are able to look beyond our inner experiences come to realize that suffering is universal.

As human beings, we can answer some of the questions that surround suffering. We can understand the psychological process of anger, the emotions that underline it, and the factors that have a correlational and causal link to committing violent acts. We can understand the scientific theories of how natural disasters like hurricanes and earthquakes occur. We can explain the physics at work in motor vehicle accidents and in tree limbs crashing to the ground. We can understand the biochemistry of the division and multiplication of cancer cells. We have voices to answer many, though certainly not all, of the how questions of tragedy. But the larger why questions of the existence of such tragic events in our world and in our personal lives are questions that are fundamentally unanswerable by all sciences—soft and hard. Suffering is one of life's ultimate questions (Crews, 1986).

Does Suffering Change Us?

It is rare to find people who have not experienced any profound stress or trauma. As we know that death is inevitable, we know that suffering must also play a part in our human development. Thus, it behooves us to ask, "Do such dark experiences hold the possibility of changing us, and more importantly, if so, then how?" The answer to the first question is a clear and unsurprising "yes." Long before the 1980s, when Posttraumatic Stress Disorder (PTSD) became a diagnosis in the *Diagnostic and Statistical Manual of Mental Disorders* III (DSM-III; American Psychiatric Association, 1980), we have been systematically studying how stress and trauma have the ability to change us in tremendously negative ways. In every realm of our existence (physical, emotional, social), trauma possesses the ability to have a profound negative impact on the human experience. This has become apparent based on extensive ongoing study of people before, during, and after trauma. The field of psychology has dedicated a great deal of resources to examining the negative outcomes.

From such a perspective, we have been primed to an awareness of the profound negative experiences and consequences of trauma. For Kelly's family and friends this meant continuing with the mundane and the milestones of their lives without the loving support of a mother, wife, sister, educator, mentor, and friend. Because of the attention and focus on the negative aspects of extreme stress and trauma, professionals are able to respond to the negative consequences of suffering in meaningful ways when working with the profound loss experienced by families and friends such as Kelly's. Research and clinical practice has focused on decreasing negative symptoms of stress and trauma, including managing the often profound, significant distress. And thankfully so.

Trauma research that focuses on the negative impacts of trauma will and should continue. Multiple levels of loss and the associated emotional distress are important aspects in the story of suffering, and they deserve great attention. However, it is becoming increasingly evident that while such focus is part of the story of stress and trauma, it is not always the entire story. A return to a premorbid state of functioning cannot always be the goal, and for some people it is not an accurate depiction of their healing process. With these factors in mind, increased attention has started to get counselors in the field to look beyond solely the negative consequences of stress and trauma.

As evidenced in Kelly's community and that of others who have experienced tragedy, sometimes the pain lifts as a new light is permitted to illuminate the darkness. For example, one of the doctoral students who Kelly was mentoring before she died wrote the following:

> I had the privilege of knowing Kelly as a professor and mentor for almost six years. As a master's-level student, I enrolled in many of her classes. Then later, as a doctoral student, I became her graduate assistant. Just prior to her death she took on the role of chair of my dissertation committee. I was grateful that she had accepted the role, and it seemed to me that she was enthusiastic about the role as well. She was to help guide me in the biggest and most important educational task ever before me. I felt great ease knowing that she would be present with me through the process. I valued her passion for education, her penchant for quality research, and the way in which she was able to encourage her mentees to produce the highest quality work possible. I could not have imagined working with anyone other than Kelly.
>
> When I heard of Kelly's death I was grief stricken, overwhelmed with the feeling of being alone. My mentor, my guide had left me. I was lost. With time, however, I came to understand something that I may never have come to know if I had not had to struggle to comprehend and make sense of Kelly's death. I realize now that true guides in our life never leave us, not even in death. Kelly was gone prematurely, yes. But her professional and personal qualities that I value so deeply were still alive in me.

And so while she was not present physically during my dissertation process, her spirit, her talent, and her wisdom were still very much accessible to me. Even after her death, she was my guide. My current recognition of who can guide and how a person may guide is a new understanding I hold about life. It is something I understand not only because of Kelly's presence in my life, but because I have had to come to accept her physical absence.

The story of Kelly's mentee reveals that positive changes can be experienced when a relationship is sought *with* the stress and trauma. Through these difficult and complicated situations, people are allowed or perhaps induced to cultivate certain positive aspects of themselves, others, and the world. This face of trauma is often ignored to the detriment of healing. In fact, we are less versed in the positive aspects of enduring stress and trauma because, until recently, the field has primarily focused its systematic rigor on the negative. Psychologists, counselors, social workers, and others trained in mental health professions were not primed to seek or foster growth but simply sought adaptation in clients; however, this approach began to change in the 1990s.

A History of Growth

In 1995 the term *posttraumatic growth* (PTG) was coined by clinical psychologists Richard Tedeschi and Lawrence Calhoun of the University of North Carolina Greensboro. Around that time other terms that spoke to a related process also began to emerge in the psychological literature: *stress-related growth* (Park, Cohen, & Murch, 1996), *benefit-finding* (Tennen & Affleck, 1998), and *adversarial growth* (Joseph, 2004; Linley & Joseph, 2004). There are important distinctions in the theories, definitions, conceptualizations, and measurements of each term, which will be highlighted shortly. However, all of the terms capture the idea that value can emerge when cognitive structures undergo the reorganization that results from experiencing stress and trauma (Joseph, 2011). The development of theories of posttraumatic growth is based both on psychological theory and on research that had been taking place for many years when the terms emerged, as well as philosophical and theological underpinnings rooted in centuries-old experiences.

From a psychological perspective, the concept of posttraumatic growth has roots in several different theoretical movements (Tedeschi & Calhoun, 1995): Caplan's Crisis Theory (1961, 1964); Rogers' client-centered theory (1961, 1964); Existential Theory (Frankl, 1963; Yalom 1980); and the Positive Psychology movement. Although ideas on human growth and potential that can result from critical life stress can be seen in other movements as well, these theories appear to have the strongest connections in the field. Each theoretical movement will be explained very briefly, with references provided for deeper exploration of the theoretical roots.

Crisis Theory

Gerald Caplan (1961, 1964) developed Crisis Theory as a result of working at Massachusetts General Hospital in the 1940s with patients who had endured severe life experiences. In his research, Caplan observed that when people experienced a crisis, their normal coping mechanisms were not useful in helping them to manage distress. The lack of an ability to successfully cope with the event led a person to experience a sense of disorganization in regard to their ability to function. In an attempt to discharge inner tensions caused by a sense of disorganization, a person in distress was led to a sort of trial-by-error attempt to end the crisis in a new way (Halpern, 1973). Such trial-by-error attempts suggest that the experience of crisis may promote the realization that one's precrisis set of coping mechanisms can be expanded beyond what one may have previously realized. Caplan's theory highlights that without crisis the need to seek new understandings about the self—namely new ways of coping—would not be identified as necessary. Seeking an expansion of coping resources comes from a place of immediate necessity when the current coping mechanisms can no longer do the job.

Existential Psychology

Posttraumatic growth is rooted in the existential movement. To fully define existential therapy is a contradiction, because it is impossible to completely capture the paradigm (Yalom, 1980). However, in general, existential psychology examines concerns that are rooted in people's existence and the dynamic conflict that arises when a person comes to confront certain realities of the human experience (Yalom, 1980). According to Yalom (1980), one of the leaders in the movement, four ultimate existential concerns result in dynamic intrapersonal conflict:

1. **Death**: Our desire to live and the nature of our finiteness
2. **Freedom**: The lack of external structure and the responsibility we have to author our own lives
3. **Isolation**: Our desire for communion and our intrinsic separateness from others
4. **Meaninglessness**: Our need for meaning in a world where it may not exist

People tend to reflect on one or more of these four ultimate concerns generally in a few situations: (a) when they are confronted with death; (b) when they have made an irreversible decision; or (c) when they experience a collapse of their meaning-making schema (Yalom, 1980). When a person gains an awareness of any of these four ultimate existential concerns, as can be the case in the wake of stress and trauma, the result is the distressing feeling of anxiety.

Depending on the severity and duration of this anxiety, it is believed that people will either move toward positive experiences of growth or negative experiences of psychopathology. Yalom's writings bring to light that, while confrontation with inner conflict can be distressing, facing one or more of the four existential concerns presents an opportunity for a person to create a new sense of meaning in life.

Victor Frankl (1963), a psychiatrist, a survivor of a Nazi concentration camp, and the founder of logotherapy, also wrote about the relationship between experiencing difficult life events and finding a sense of meaning in order to transcend what Frankl considers to be the intrinsic pain of human existence. In *Man's Search for Meaning*, he writes: "To live is to suffer, to survive is to find meaning in the suffering" (p. 11). Frankl believed that life is essentially meaningless until a person gives it meaning. Central to Frankl's argument is that a person is able to find meaning in every situation that is presented to the human experience, including those that are extremely tragic. According to Frankl (1963), meaning cannot be acquired from another person. Rather, an individual has free will and a responsibility to give life meaning in each moment; for "meaning in life differs from man to man, from moment to moment" (p. 98).

Seen in the two examples of existential writings is the idea that while suffering is an inevitable part of human existence, finding new meaning through confrontation with painful life events is indeed possible, and perhaps even the ultimate goal. Although death, for example, cannot be escaped, it can be confronted, and through an awareness of the confrontation, one may choose to live life differently, with new meaning and purpose not understood before facing a confrontation with death.

Rogers's Person-Centered Approach

A third figure to influence the present-day movements of post-traumatic growth is Carl Rogers, founder of the person-centered approach to therapy. The work of Carl Rogers is based on the premise that human beings are intrinsically designed to, and motivated toward, growth. Rogers's Organismic Valuing Process Theory (1964) articulates that it is a normal, natural tendency for an individual to move toward meaning-making and growth *if* one's social environment supports a person in doing so (Joseph & Linley, 2006). Growth conceived as a basic motivation does not necessarily equate to growth experienced by all individuals. A hostile society and adverse circumstances can cause anxiety and fear, which can turn people away from maturity and the development of authentic selves. However, when a person experiences authenticity, competence, and relatedness in the social environment, a person's natural tendency to move toward growth and actualization becomes more likely (Joseph & Linley, 2006). One might say that according to Rogers, humans were designed to grow.

Positive Psychology

Major influences to the current conceptualizations of growth are rooted in positive psychology, a movement named by Martin Seligman, 1998 American Psychological Association president (Peterson, 2006). A traditional psychological frame, as opposed to the positive psychological frame, focuses on symptomology and problems. The key question asked by traditional psychology is that of, "What is going wrong?" However, in the positive psychology movement, questions center on resilience and what strengths a person has that support not only overcoming an obstacle, but also flourishing as a result. In this way, positive psychology attempts to claim a sense of balance (Maddux, 2002) by asking the often-overlooked question, "What is going right?" The positive psychological approach considers what is working by seeking to understand what cannot be understood and by accessing what cannot be accessed in the human story when *only* a symptomological approach is used. The way questions are framed provides a limit and boundary with which to seek an answer. We will never understand what is going right and why it is going right when we only ask symptom-based questions.

One particular aspect of positive psychology that is useful when considering posttraumatic growth is the different way in which positive psychology has examined well-being. Traditional psychology often explores hedonic well-being, perhaps the more commonly understood form of well-being or happiness, which is concerned with decreasing the amount of negative affect and increasing the amount of positive affect that a person experiences. Positive psychology has brought increased focus to eudaimonic well-being. *Eudaimonia* is a Greek term that Aristotle used to describe the good life or living well. This type of well-being or happiness is focused more on increasing meaning, purpose, actualization, authenticity, and growth in an attempt to capture more closely the experience of psychological flourishing. The two different types of well-being are not on a continuum but rather are separate philosophies. It has been suggested that in order to understand posttraumatic growth and the good that it offers, hedonia can be a starting point, but the definition of well-being must be expanded to include the ideas of thinking deeply and living well (Calhoun & Tedeschi, 2006), which are more commonly associated with eudaimonia. Increased attention on eudaimonic well-being, as opposed to hedonic well-being, allows for a broader understanding of struggle and trauma that is arguably a more complete picture of the human experience (Joseph, 2011).

Present-Day Study of Growth

In the mid 1990s, the research base for posttraumatic growth was just formally building. By the mid 2000s, the empirical research base on the construct of growth was increasing. In 2005, ninety-five articles on *posttraumatic growth* were available in the Psych Info database, and an additional 33 articles appeared when the term *stress-related growth* was considered (Calhoun & Tedeschi, 2006) in the search. At that time resources on posttraumatic growth were also included in the texts by Calhoun and Tedeschi: *Trauma and Transformation* (1995); *Facilitating Posttraumatic Growth: A Clinician's Guide* (1999); and *The Handbook of Posttraumatic Growth* (2006). Tedeschi and Calhoun were also joined by Park in the 1998 book *Posttraumatic Growth: Positive Changes in the Aftermath of Crisis.*

By 2011, a query of *posttraumatic growth* produced roughly 350 articles from the Psych Info database and expanded to nearly 500 when the term *stress-related growth* was included. Several texts were also added. In 2008, Joseph and Linley wrote the book *Trauma, Recovery, and Growth: Positive Psychological Perspectives on Posttraumatic Stress.* In 2009, Park, Lechner, and Antoni edited a book geared toward understanding medical illness and growth, *Medical Illness and Positive Life Change: Can Crisis Lead to Personal Transformation?* Most recently, *Posttraumatic Growth and Culturally Competent Practice: Lessons Learned from Around the Globe* by Weiss and Berger (2010) and *What Doesn't Kill Us: The New Psychology of Posttraumatic Growth* by Joseph (2011) were added to the literature as well. However, the current literature is certainly predominantly for researchers, with some articles and chapters either specifically focused on or including clinical implications of the research, but very few works are dedicated completely to clinicians as the primary audience.

Conceptualizations and Definitions of Posttraumatic Growth

As previously mentioned, Tedeschi and Calhoun developed the phrase *posttraumatic growth* in 1995 to refer to the positive psychological changes that a person experiences as a result of enduring stress and trauma. Several other terms have also been used to refer to the same or similar constructs. Some overlap occurs between models and terms, but there are important distinctions in the definitions and models of growth as well.

Tedeschi and Calhoun's definition and conceptualization of posttraumatic growth highlights the profound nature of the stressful experience. The idea of posttraumatic growth is anchored in distress that reaches far beyond everyday stressors (Tedeschi & Calhoun, 2004), speaking instead of the forms of distress that may lead to a sort of *assumptive* transformation within the self. For the phenomena of posttraumatic growth to occur, a person must experience a significant level of disruption to their assumptive world and personal narrative (Calhoun & Tedeschi, 2006) in a way that alters a person's experience of everyday life. In a meeting of psychologists at the 2005 American Psychological Association Science Directorate conference on Positive Life Changes in the Context of Medical Illness, a group of experts gathered to flush out the differences in some of the terms related to posttraumatic growth (Park, 2009). The group identified that the term *posttraumatic growth* and the mechanism associated with it suggest a *radical* reconstruction of a person's life as a result of rebuilding assumptions that are shattered by trauma.

Calhoun and Tedeschi's model of posttraumatic growth was first presented in 1995 and later revived in 2004. It is perhaps the most widely recognized and researched model of growth in the literature. The model, a development of Schaefer and Moos's (1992) model of personal growth, is integrative in that stress and coping are understood as related to personal, environmental, social, and cultural factors that influence the response that a person has to traumatic life events. According to Tedeschi & Calhoun (1995), a person's response to trauma is understood to be part of a complex system of feedback loops. The model takes into account the bidirectional relationship between a number of different factors, which include:

- Characteristics of the person
- Characteristics of the circumstances
- Management of emotional distress

- Automatic and deliberate process of rumination/cognitive engagement
- Self-disclosure
- Societal and cultural influences
- Narrative development
- Wisdom (Calhoun & Tedeschi, 2006, p. 9)

A great deal of the research base comes from either Calhoun and Tedeschi directly or other researchers examining their model.

Crystal Park developed the meaning-making model of coping, a second model that provides evidence for how growth may occur from stress or trauma. In Park's work, she uses the language *stress-related growth* rather than posttraumatic growth, allowing for a broader understanding of what types of events and amounts of distress are needed for a person to engage in a process of growth. The change associated with stress-related growth may be understood as less radical and dramatic than change captured by posttraumatic growth, and because of this stress-related growth is thought to be more common than posttraumatic growth (Park, 2009).

Park's model, a development of Lazarus and Folkman's (1987) transactional model of stress and coping, is based on the cognitive appraisals that people make during stressful events and the coping strategies that follow their appraisals (Park, 2005a). Park's model is contextual in that it focuses on the situational-based factors that direct people's choices in coping (Holahan, Moos, & Schaefer, 1996). Park argues that coping research traditionally highlights the role of problem-solving or emotion-focused coping after a stressful event has been experienced. In difficult situations, individuals attempt to analyze possible solutions or manage emotional distress. However, when a person experiences traumatic life events, coping is necessarily different in nature, demanding the acquisition of new meaning in the unsolvable or irreparable situations of trauma.

Park understands growth as that which comes from the meaning-making process, the search for comprehensibility and significance after a stressful life event. Meaning is found through reappraising either the stressor or one's global beliefs and goals. The meaning-making process is initiated by the distress experienced from a person's two conflicting belief systems: (1) the global beliefs held about the world and (2) the situational belief that has been assigned to the stressful event. In an effort to decrease the distress experienced between two conflicting belief systems, a person may come to create new global meaning. Sometimes in the search for meaning-making, a person may create meaning that is negative (e.g., believing that stress or trauma happens because he or she is a person unworthy of good). However, sometimes the new meaning created is positive, in which case growth experiences may occur.

A third model of growth following adversity is provided by Stephen Joseph (2004) and his work with Peter Linley. Joseph and Linley use the term *adversarial growth* to speak about the positive changes that a person experiences as a result of experiencing stress and trauma. The theory that drives Joseph's model is quite different in that it is an antimedical humanistic integrative approach to the idea of posttraumatic growth (Joseph, 2011). Whereas Calhoun and Tedeschi's and Park's models come from theories that are functional-descriptive, Joseph's (2004) model comes from a theory that is person-centered and based on Rogers's (1964) Organismic Value Processing Theory (Joseph & Linley, 2006). Joseph suggests, as Rogers's work did, that under a supportive social environment, growth is a natural, intrinsic human motivation and tendency. Joseph's work seeks to normalize posttraumatic stress as a breakdown and disorganization of the self-structure. Through the breakdown of the self-structure and reorganization of a new self-structure that is congruent with the stressful or traumatic experience, a person moves more closely toward the experience that Rogers (1959) defined as "fully-functioning." In the words of Joseph and Linley:

> The fully functioning person is someone who is accepting of themselves, values all aspects of themselves—their strengths and their weaknesses—is able to live fully in the present, experiences life as a process, finds purpose and meaning in life, desires authenticity in themselves, others, and societal organizations, values deep trusting relationships and is compassionate toward others, is able to receive compassion from others, and is acceptant that change is necessary and inevitable. (Joseph & Linley, 2006, p. 1044)

Based on a person's social environmental context, there are three possible ways of cognitively reorganizing a stressful and traumatic experience, and as such three separate possible outcomes. According to Joseph and Linley (2006), after experiencing stress or trauma, a person may:

1. Assimilate the information into a preexisting self-state and so return to a pretrauma level of functioning, as such leaving a person vulnerable to retraumatization
2. Accommodate the information in negative ways, which will result in experiences of psychopathology and the accompanied distress
3. Accommodate the information in positive ways, which will lead to growth experiences

In the literature, the terms *posttraumatic growth, stress-related growth*, and *adversarial growth*, though having different hypothesized definitions and mechanisms through which the experience is achieved, at times are used interchangeably. In fact, meta-analyses on positive changes following stress and trauma have included studies that use all three definitions and conceptualizations (as well as others). They all certainly attempt to capture the once-neglected positive experiences that may result from a person enduring intrinsically negative experiences. From historical, research, and clinical perspectives, however, it is important to recognize both the similarities and the differences in the conceptualizations of growth following stress and trauma. Further reading of primary texts from the authors is quite useful for the clinician wishing to deeply understand the concepts of growth following stress and trauma.

Measurement of Growth

Valid and reliable measurement is a cornerstone of empirical research. By the mid- to late 1990s, several measures had been developed and were beginning to build the evidence of validity: the Changes in Outlook Questionnaire (Joseph, Williams & Yule, 1993); the Posttraumatic Growth Inventory (Tedeschi & Calhoun, 1996); the Stress-Related Growth Inventory (Park, Cohen, & Murch, 1996); and the Perceived Benefits Scale (McMillen & Fisher, 1998). There is empirical support for the adequate reliability and validity of each of these measures. (For a more detailed further reading on the reliability and validity of each instrument, see Joseph and Linley, 2008, as well as the original citation for each scale.)

Joseph, Williams, and Yule (1993) developed the Changes in Outlook Questionnaire, a 26-item measure to assess both the positive and negative ways a stressful or traumatic event changed a person's view of life. In the measure, 11 items assess positive changes (e.g., "I value my relationships much more now"), and 15 items measure negative changes (e.g., "I don't look forward to the future anymore"). Items are measured on a 6-point Likert-type scale ranging from 1 = *Strongly agree* to 6 = *Strongly disagree*. The scale was developed using a sample of 35 adult survivors of a cruise ship accident in which an oil tanker collided with a ship carrying 400 schoolchildren and

90 teachers and other adults, causing the ship to rapidly take on water and list. Four people died in the incident: one child, one teacher, and two seamen. The authors asked two questions of the adult survivors to assess if the disaster changed their view of life for the better or for the worse, and how. The open-ended responses were then rated by five graduate psychologists. The responses that were unanimously positive or negative were then used as the preliminary measure of changes in outlook. A 10-item short form of the scale was later developed by Joseph, Linley, Shevlin, Goodfellow, and Butler (2006).

Tedeschi and Calhoun (1996) developed the Posttraumatic Growth Inventory, a 21-item measure used to assess "the extent to which survivors of traumatic events perceive personal benefits, including changes in perceptions of self, relationships with others, and philosophy of life, accruing from their attempts to cope with trauma and its aftermath" (p. 458). The scale consists of five subscales: Relating to Others; New Possibilities; Personal Strength; Spiritual Change; and Appreciation for Life. A total score and subscale scores can be calculated from the measure. Items are scored on a 6-point Likert-type scale ranging from 0 = *I did not experience this change as a result of my crisis* to 5 = *I experienced this change to a great degree as a result of my crisis*. The scale was developed by first reviewing the literature for reported positive changes after traumatic events and examined using a sample of 199 male and 405 female undergraduate students who reported to have experienced a significant negative life event in the 5 years before the study. Cann et al. (2010) developed a 10-item short form, which consists of two items from each of the aforementioned subscales.

Park et al. (1996) developed the Stress-Related Growth Scale, a 50-item self-report measure, to capture positive changes following an identified stressful event in four areas: personal resources, social relationships, life philosophy, and coping skills. Items are answered on a 3-point frequency scale: 0 = *Not at all*, 1 = *Somewhat*, and 2 = *A great deal*. Sample items include "I started a deep and meaningful relationship with another," "I learned that I want to have some impact on the world," and "I learned better ways to express my feelings."

The Stress-Related Growth Scale was developed in a sample comprising 506 college students. Participants were asked to identify a negative stressful event that they experienced within 12 months and then to respond to 82 items referencing personal growth. A total of 32 items were deleted because of skewed responses, amounting the 50-item scale. A 15-item short form of the scale was developed by Cohen, Hettler, and Pane (1998). It consists of the 15 highest-loading items of the 50-item measure.

McMillen and Fisher (1998) developed the Perceived Benefits Scale, which measures the perceived changes in a person's life as a result of a negative life experience. The scale consists of 30 items that assess positive gain and eight items that assess negative gain. The scale includes eight subscales: enhanced self-efficacy (e.g., "This event made me a stronger person"); increased community close-ness (e.g., "Because of this event, I know my neighbors better"); increased spirituality (e.g., "Because of this event, I am more spiri-tual"); increased compassion (e.g., "Because of this event, I am more compassionate to those in similar situations"); increased faith in other people (e.g., "Because of this event, I realized how good peo-ple can be"); increased family closeness (e.g., "Because of this event, I am closer to the people I care about"); lifestyle changes (e.g., " As a result of this event, I live more for the moment"); and material gain (e.g., "I gained financially because of this event"). Responses range from 0 = *Not at all like my experience* to 4 = *Very much like my experience*. Scale items were developed from open-ended responses to questions on changes that occurred from an identified traumatic event in a person's life. The scale was first examined in a community sample of 289 adult spectators at a children's baseball game. No short form of the scale currently exists.

Two important notes need to be made in regard to measure-ment. First, it should be noted that all of the measures that exist to assess growth following stress and trauma are self-report measures. This matter has led to some debate in the field as to whether the instruments can truly measure observable growth. The limitation of self-report measures such as these is that the possibility exists that what is being measured are perceived changes and not actual changes (see Chapter 2 for a more detailed review of this question). Secondly, there is empirical research to support that the various measures are correlated but not identical. With this in mind, researchers have suggested that if a measure is to be used clinically, then clinicians should consider not relying on one measure alone but rather may desire to give several measures to be certain to have a more complete understanding of a person's experience of growth following stress and trauma (Joseph & Linley, 2008).

Who Experiences Growth?

An important clinical question to consider is that of who may experience growth following stress and trauma. The simple answer to the question is that any of our clients, their family members, and friends could adapt and become wiser in the process of enduring stress and trauma. The reality is that not everyone will. Prevalence rates reported for posttraumatic growth have a large range that depends on the study. Davis, Nolen-Hoeksema, and Larson (1998) report that rates of posttraumatic growth range from 3% to 40% in a sample of bereaved individuals. Frazier, Conlon, and Glaser (2001) report a range of 20% to 80% for female sexual assault survivors. Weiss (2002) reports a rate of 98% in a sample of women with breast cancer. Harms and Talbot (2007) reported that 99% of the sample experienced posttraumatic growth at an Australian rehabilitation center where the sample of 79 patients had experienced a serious orthopedic injury 3 to 4 years prior to the study.

Studies have cast a wide net in regard to sample participants in an attempt to better understand the generalizability of the phenomena.

A meta-analysis by Helgeson, Reynolds, and Tomich (2006) on posttraumatic growth in 26 studies that included 7,113 participants suggests that women are more likely to find benefits after stressful experiences. Additionally, in the same meta-analysis, a total of eight studies and 1,281 participants suggest that nonwhites are also more likely than whites to find benefits after trauma. Such findings are not to suggest that clinicians should only consider nonwhite women clients as potential candidates for growth following stress and trauma.

Turning to the nature of the stressful or traumatic event, evidence is mounting now that posttraumatic growth may be experienced by persons experiencing such diverse trauma and the extreme stress that is part and parcel of HIV/AIDS (Cadell & Sullivan, 2006); cancer (Cordova, Cunningham, Carlson, & Andrykowski, 2001; Tomich & Helgeson, 2006); bereavement (Engelkemeyer & Marwit, 2008); physical and sexual assault (Grubaugh & Resick, 2007); physical illness (Helgeson et al., 2006); traumatic brain injury (McGrath & Linley, 2006); serious orthopedic injury (Harms & Talbot, 2007); or 9/11-type terrorist attacks (Ai, Cascio, Santangelo, & Evans-Campball, 2005). Evidence of posttraumatic growth across many different types of events makes it clear that other event characteristics may be even more important than the event itself.

For instance, it has been speculated that the individual characteristics of a person who experiences an event may be of greater concern than the type of event. Calhoun and Tedeschi (2006) suggest that experiencing growth may be linked to a person's coping abilities before the time of stress or trauma. Specifically, if a person has too few coping abilities, he or she may be too weak to experience growth. However, if one has too many coping abilities, he or she may be resistant to growth after stress and trauma.

Additionally, the level of distress that a person experiences as a result of the event has been examined as a more important factor for understanding whom may experience growth, rather than the event type. Research has presented what appears to be a curvilinear upside-down U-shaped relationship between stress and growth, not a linear relationship (Levine, Laufer, Hamama-Raz, Stein, & Soloman, 2008). The findings suggest that growth is greater for those with moderate adjustment to stress—those who are *not resilient to*, but also not flooded by, stress. It seems that we need our assumptive worlds to be radically shaken if not shattered (Janoff-Bulman, 1992) if we are to initiate rebuilding them

Take, for example, the case of Andrew, a 53-year-old man whose father died of cancer at 87 years old. When his father was diagnosed 3 years prior, Andrew experienced a sense of great sadness. For all of his life, Andrew looked to his father as a guide and a mentor. Andrew had very fond memories of yearly fishing trips that he took with his father when Andrew was a young boy. His father, a skilled engineer, was who Andrew turned to when he struggled in high school and college math classes. When Andrew married his wife, his father gave a toast encouraging Andrew to celebrate the big moments such as weddings with all his heart, but to not take for granted the everyday moments in life; for the small moments need all of one's heart too. Andrew recollected at his father's funeral that while he may have never told his father, he held those words close to his heart on that day, and still did now.

When Andrew's first son was born, he named him after his father. When he told his father the name of his son, it was a moment that Andrew remembers brought tears to his father's eyes. Andrew recalled his father as a man who lived with great love, great compassion, and great wisdom. The death of Andrew's father brought with it great sadness for Andrew. He missed his father deeply; however, the sadness that he felt was accompanied too by an understanding of death as part of life. He had experienced several losses in his life prior to his father's death. Some of his experience, like the death of his older brother in a motor vehicle accident some 30 years prior, caused such darkness he wondered if he would ever come to see light again in his life. In fact, his father helped Andrew to reclaim his life after the death of his brother. This same darkness was not present in Andrew's experience of the death of his father. His assumptive world was not shattered by his father's death. He felt heartbroken and empty in moments. He felt loss and sadness. Still, the death of his father was comprehensible to Andrew. Although there were the occasional moments when he felt the urge to pick up the phone and call his father, or remind himself that he wanted to tell his father something, the death of his father made sense to him.

The example of Andrew, however, can be contrasted with the example of Melissa, a 23-year-old college student who, for several reasons, was raised by her grandparents from the time she was 12 years old. When it was time to graduate high school and consider college, Melissa's grandparents encouraged her to stay local. Her grandparents liked taking care of Melissa, and Melissa admittedly liked being taken care of by her grandparents. She recalled that she had a special relationship with her grandmother, who filled a void left by her mother, who had abandoned her when she was 3 years old. The decision to stay local was easy. Melissa found a job working at a local retail store and started taking classes at a nearby college part time.

One Saturday morning, Melissa's grandmother went to the store to pick up a few groceries. When her grandmother did not come back after an hour, Melissa started to worry. She frantically drove to the grocery store in search of her grandmother. Later, Melissa would learn that while she was shopping, Melissa's grandmother started to feel unwell. She was taken to a nearby hospital by a neighbor and friend who happened to be shopping there as well. However, en route to the hospital, Melissa's grandmother experienced a heart attack and was declared dead within minutes of her arrival. There was nothing the medical community could have done to change the outcome.

Melissa struggled intensely to comprehend her grandmother's death; she could not imagine a life without her grandmother. She remembered feeling as though the world as she knew it had crumbled before her eyes as she attempted to mourn the loss of her grandmother, and the void that she had from the loss of her mother reopened again. Melissa faced for the first time the existential question of death and faced feelings of lack of meaning and purpose in life.

These two examples of adults facing the experience of the death of a grandparent illustrate that life events are dynamic and personal. To develop a list of people who will and those who will not grow based on the event alone is unreliable. For some, the death of a loved one can shatter one's assumptive world. For others, it may not. A more important clinical question then when assessing for the possibility of growth may not be what is the event that a person experienced, but how much distress did the event cause? And what is the sociocultural context in which the event took place?

We can never remove a person from their context; therefore, a deep understanding of sociocultural influences on a person is essential. Clinicians realize that, in the end, for as universal as stress and trauma is, healing occurs at the individual level. Clinicians work with people who have experienced trauma and who may grow from those situations. The research tells us about the likelihood of the relationships that exist between trauma and growth. Clients can reflect on these relationships and offer their insights into their value. As clinicians, we must remain open so our expectations of growth do not cause clients further distress (Wortman, 2004). Likewise, clinicians must not restrict the nature of the life events that may shatter one's assumptive world and bring one face to face with the existential questions of life.

Three Images of Trauma and Growth

In working with clients, over time, some clinicians may start to become aware of growth experiences. This book is geared toward the client's seedlings of awareness. To this end, three images may be useful for a therapist to hold when working with clients.

The first image that is important for the therapist to hold is that of the wreckage associated with stress and trauma. In this era of technological advances, people are bombarded with photos, videos, and instant messages that often provide real-time views of natural disasters and human violence, and there have been many: the massive destruction of the tornadoes that swept across the Midwestern United States in April 2011 killing 346 people; the devastation of the Haitian earthquake of January 2010 that left many still living in tent cities more than a year later; the 2008 tsunami that wiped away cities and generations of families in Japan; and the terrorist attacks of September 11, 2001, in New York, Washington, D.C., and Pennsylvania. Common to all of these examples are the images of scattered debris representing the only remnants of homes, offices, and shopping areas, and the many faces distorted by anguish and grief. In each instance, there was a "before" and now there is an "after."

These remnants are negative, violent, destructive, and dark. They hold within them tragic individual life narratives. The splintered wood was not merely a house, but a home. It may have contained the space of Christmas mornings, first steps, and lazy Sunday afternoons. There may have been a favorite chair, book, or stuffed animal that beckoned daily attention. The wreckage claimed mothers, fathers, sisters, brothers, wives, husbands, neighbors, children, colleagues, and friends. It claimed familiarity, predictability, and the definitive sense of knowing how the world operates. Holding such an image in general—and, when working with a client, holding their intrinsically negative image—is important. This is what clients first seek: for someone else to hold this image to decrease the isolation of holding it themselves.

Important in the study of the area of posttraumatic growth is the understanding that trauma must inherently be understood as negative. Trauma and suffering are not to be glorified or sugar-coated.

As the research literature has found, trauma has profoundly negative impacts on an individual, community, and global level. On the individual level, extreme stress and trauma may result in profound experiences of distress. The *DSM-IV-TR*'s (APA, 2000) definition of Posttraumatic Stress Disorder identifies three areas characteristic of traumatic responses: (1) intrusive recollection—reexperiencing the traumatic events through thoughts and flashbacks; (2) avoidance/numbing; and (3) hyperarousal. The experience of posttraumatic stress can be understood to range from mild to severe based on individual reactions. One need not meet the disorder criteria to still experience distress for which one seeks counseling.

First and foremost, clients seek therapy to help manage their distress with the hopes of full alleviation. They do not come seeking definitions of posttraumatic growth. There are several essential elements to treating trauma including:

- Desensitization
- Creating a narrative that makes sense of the incidents or at least makes them understandable in some way
- Recreating a sense of safety
- Recreating a worldview that encompasses what happened as well as a functional life post trauma (Calhoun & Tedeschi, 1999, p. 53)

Clinicians who wish to understand the clinical implications of the research of posttraumatic growth would be remiss if they attempted to take growth out of the context of suffering. To understand growth, clinicians must first understand and be able to hold an image of suffering.

With a full realization of suffering, the second image presented that a therapist must hold is the image of growth that a client will not hold at first (and some not at all). Growth is an image of one *reaching upward*. Many have experienced this sensation of elevation, which is often attached to a striving toward something. It is a singularly human feature that represents movement, has a cadence, and is at the essence of being alive. We have seen images of rising—Olympic medalists making their way to the awards stand, mountain climbers approaching summits, and astronauts steering a space shuttle toward the far reaches of the galaxy. Images of reaching upward are filled with promise and hope; they capture the triumph in a life narrative. It is not the therapist's job or goal to supply such an image. It is the therapist's job to be open to a belief that such an image may start to become real for a client. And when it does, it is the therapist's job to honor that image as a part of the client.

The final and most relevant image that is important for therapists to hold is that of *the potential relationship between the destruction and reaching upward, between the darkness and the light.* It is only because of the wreckage left by the destruction of trauma that people have before them a place to climb and in the climbing they may come to gain a new vantage point, thereby helping them to obtain a new perspective. The world has not changed, but their sadness and woundedness changes their experience of life. This paradoxical relationship is at the heart of posttraumatic growth. For therapists to be able to work with growth, they must understand the complex relationship between darkness and light. If complexity is not valued in the relationship, then platitudes may be sought or expressed with no benefit whatsoever to the client.

The paradox of posttraumatic growth is not about merely having a positive reframe of the trauma (Neimeyer, 2001), which would be akin to putting a bandage on a gaping wound, but a deliberate exploration and willingness to reexamine life within this new context—including the traumatic event. Throughout the process of gaining self-insight, there must be a way to hold the negative event. In time and with great patience, there must be a way to draw out that which is positive so healing can begin. This does not mean that a dark, angry sky should be naively painted a happy blue, but instead that the depths of clouds and the breakthrough of the occasional sunbeam change those who look at it.

Clinicians must work with the cognitive debris that is the result of stress and trauma. Clients may be able to go through the outward motions of operating in this "after" and become stuck, whereas others may shut down completely and hide themselves away and yet others will embrace the journey. For any movement to occur, previously held assumptions of how their life stories were supposed to be written, no matter how they started or what came before, must be reevaluated.

When a situational traumatic experience occurs, assumptions about the world as meaningful, benevolent, and good are obliterated (Janoff-Bulman, 1992). Thus a cognitive frame must be introduced so the experiences can once again be processed. New beliefs about how the world works must be hypothesized, tested, and used. A new normal must be the anchor from which to operate going forward. To ignore this basic premise would mean continued distress. In some way, we need to reclaim such assumptions, but we must hold them in more complex ways.

Conclusions

In his 1932 book, *Night Flight,* Antoine de Saint-Exupery wrote, "Even our misfortunes are part of our belongings." Saint-Exupery's words speak to the reality that a person may hold both painful and joyful experiences in an integrated way as part of the human existence. To this end, we as clinicians need to study growth. We need to be aware of growth. We need to know what growth looks like. But we must also be very careful not to *need* growth in our clients. If we need it, we risk harming not only the process but also the person. Buddhist psychology tells us that a beneficial stance to take is one of acceptance: in other words, prizing people for whom and what they are while calling them to be all they can be.

Although this is a psychologically framed book, it is noteworthy to state that psychologists did not invent the idea of new growth becoming possible after trauma that might never have evidenced itself if the serious stressor had never occurred. The idea is rooted in the narrative of the human experience. What psychological researchers have done is to define the experience, and they have been (and currently are) measuring the experience in order to increase knowledge and move closer to a fuller understanding around the idea. They have been and are attempting to answer the who, what, where, when, and why of growth. Naming the phenomena and answering the aforementioned questions does not make the experience any more or less real, but it can better inform us about the intricacies of the relationship between the trauma experience and its impact on mental health and flourishing. None of this study is focused on negating the negative impact of trauma. Trauma is intrinsically negative. To take the conversation out of the context of suffering would do a great disservice to the client and to the conversation at hand. However, to not include growth in clinicians' conversations of suffering is a disservice as well.

There is a long way to go in this area of research. In some ways, when examined from a comparative standpoint to the database of information that exists on the negative experiences of trauma, we are only at the beginning. On the other hand, there exists almost 20 years of research in the specific area of posttraumatic growth and even more in the areas where posttraumatic growth is rooted. So while an argument has been made of the premature nature of the expansion in clinical work on posttraumatic growth, so too an argument exists that the experience has been happening for as long as therapy has existed and in theology before that.

Psychology invented the term, not the phenomena. People are talking about growth and taking the movement to a new place. The relief of symptoms is part of what clients seek. Yet what each person comes to understand is that the posttrauma world is a one-way ticket, and there are no returns to the previous way of life. We cannot move backward. Cognitive slides backward do not move people back to a pretrauma world. Only when the earnest desire to reclaim a pretrauma life is abandoned is there hope for a new life.

When we fall, do we get up? And if we get up, do we get to an up experience that is cognitively and emotionally different than where we were before we and our physical and assumptive worlds fell down? And within this sense of newness is there anything positive? Or is it merely negative or neutral? These are fundamental questions of the work of stress and growth.

Posttraumatic growth advocates do not presume in any way that new and different experiences, understandings, or perspectives are always positive, but sometimes pieces of them are. Accordingly, the study of posttraumatic growth is not a comparison of pre- and post-lives in the sense that one is better or worse. Instead, it is the study of coming to terms and accepting what is different and about questioning the piece or pieces that are different and determining if they have intrinsically positive qualities that are worthy of being honored for what they are. When these qualities are honored, amazing results become truly possible. Such honoring may begin when we as clinicians and caregivers learn to offer our clients a culture that believes in the possibility of growth.

A Quote to Remember

When the individual is able to engage in disclosures that contain themes of growth, when the growth themes are part of the narratives and idioms of the proximate culture's narrative and idioms related to posttraumatic response, and when disclosures are met with accepting or affirming responses from significant others, then growth is more likely to be experienced. (Tedeschi & Calhoun, 2006, p. 14)

Clinical Cornerstones of the Chapter

- As clinicians we hear many "why" questions associated with people's suffering. This is an understandable part of the initial process of coming to terms with dramatic disruptive post-traumatic growth, the impact on one's worldview. However, in order for people to experience posttraumatic growth, the search for a reason needs to be abandoned in favor of using that energy to explore new ways of viewing themselves and the world given the occurrence of the trauma.

- The concept of posttraumatic growth is rooted in theological and philosophical traditions, so there is much to be gained by reading Frankl, Yalom, and other existentialists, as well as the writings of contemporary atheistic (Buddhist) and theistic (Jewish, Christian, Hindu) writings on suffering and compassion.

- A paradoxical relationship is at the heart of posttraumatic growth. The ability to understand the paradox is an essential element to understanding the definition of posttraumatic growth.

- Posttraumatic growth does not occur by simply seeking and finding a positive reframe of trauma (Neimeyer, 2001). Instead, one must be able to find a way to honor an event as negative while being open to those signs that might indicate the client is enduring the stress in new ways or even growing in previously unforeseen ways.

- Recognize that clients, family members, and their friends can experience growth from a traumatic experience; however, not everyone does and nor should be expected to by the clinician.

- The type of the event alone is not an indicator of who will and who will not grow. The process is individual and dynamic. Thus, it is more profitable for the clinician to know how much distress the event *caused the client* instead of the nature of the event.

- If clinicians have an expectation of growth in their clients, then they may cause only further distress to the client

(Wortman, 2004). Consequently, the delicate balance requires being open to potential new growth (instead of framing it only as denial or avoidance) while not pacing the sessions too fast or providing feedback that indicates to clients they are failures if they don't experience posttraumatic growth. For some, a successful therapeutic experience will be a return to a premorbid phase of functioning; for others, new insight and wisdom will occur. Counselors who are familiar with posttraumatic growth are better able to guide both types of clients.

Selected References

Calhoun, L., & Tedeschi, R. (Eds.). (2006). *Handbook on posttraumatic growth: Research and practice*. Mahwah, NJ: Erlbaum.
This text was edited by the researchers who coined the term *posttraumatic growth*. The book provides an overview of the research and related implications for practice relative to posttraumatic growth up to the year 2006.
Janoff-Bulman, R. (1992). *Shattered assumptions*. New York, NY: Free Press.
Foundational reading on psychological trauma that highlights how a person's global assumptions of meaning, benevolence, and worth may be shattered by traumatic events, and the need individuals have to rebuild fundamental global assumptions that reclaim such themes.
Holahan, C., Moos, R., & Schaefer, J. (1996). Coping, stress resistance, and growth: Conceptualizing adaptive functioning. In M. Zeidner & N. S. Endler (Eds.), *Handbook of coping* (pp. 24–43). Hoboken, NJ: Wiley.
A chapter overview of the relationship between coping, stress, and growth, which highlights foundational work that

influenced Tedeschi and Calhouns's current model of posttraumatic growth.

Joseph, S. (2011). *What doesn't kill us: The new psychology of posttraumatic growth*. New York, NY: Basic Books.

A presentation from one of the leading researchers in the area of posttraumatic growth that articulates a paradigm that normalizes posttraumatic stress as part of the adaption process that serves as "an engine of transformation." The text includes clinically relevant material such as the Psychological Well-Being Post-Trauma Change Questionnaire (PWB-PTCQ) and the TRIVE model that specifies a six-stage process of how change occurs, complete with exercises and reflections.

Joseph, S., & Linley, P. (2008). *Trauma, recovery, and growth: Positive psychological perspectives on posttraumatic stress*. Hoboken, NJ: Wiley.

An edited work that provides a comprehensive look at various aspects of relationships between trauma and growth.

CHAPTER 2

POSTTRAUMATIC GROWTH: TRUTH OR MYTH?

Some research experts have questioned the veracity of the concept of posttraumatic growth. The controversy centers on the argument of whether the subjective experience of posttraumatic growth is a reality or merely an illusionary account (Sumalla et al., 2009). Measurements that exist to capture growth, such as the Posttraumatic Growth Inventory (Tedeschi & Calhoun, 1996), the Stress-Related Growth Inventory (Park, Cohen, & Murch, 1996), and the like, are self-report measures; as such they ask people to recall and compare aspects about themselves from two different points in time: pre- and posttrauma. Subjective accounts may not necessarily equate to objective experiences of growth, raising the following questions in regards to the use of self-report measures and what the field actually knows about growth:

- Do people, as good-intentioned and honest as they attempt to be, possess the capacity to accurately judge how they have changed over time (Gunty et al., 2011)?
- Could the experience of growth merely be a means of cognitively avoiding the processing of painful traumatic events?
- Is the experience of trauma one that drops the level of functioning to a decreased, posttrauma level? So, then, is growth simply a return to a baseline, pretrauma level of functioning that is accurately claimed as positive but inaccurately believed to be new?

- Or, are people truly experiencing something positive and new as a result of enduring and processing the extreme stress and trauma they have encountered as conceptualized by theories of growth following stress and trauma?

One of the most robust ways of accumulating evidence to prove that growth is real entails longitudinal studies that follow people pre- and posttrauma. In part, questions such as those mentioned previously exist because obtaining pretrauma data can understandably be quite difficult (Ransom, Sheldon, & Jacobsen, 2008). Several approaches, however, can be utilized to find evidence to support growth as veridical, growth as illusionary, or both. For instance, evidence could be accumulated to support growth as illusionary if those who indicate posttraumatic growth also evidence the use of defense mechanisms or cognitive avoidance as a means to reduce their psychological distress and nothing more (Sumalla et al., 2009). A certain level of evidence for the veracity of growth is possible to evidence by corroborating self-report data from people based on their own experience of growth with observer report data, perhaps from a parent, close friend, partner, or spouse who knew them both pre- and posttrauma. To some degree, both of these approaches have been used in the research literature.

The Functional Nature of Growth as an Illusion

The question of the veracity of growth, and the related limitations of self-report measures, brings to light not only the obvious question of whether the posttraumatic growth that people report is actual or perceived but also the question of whether if growth is merely perception, if that perception is functioning in adaptive or maladaptive ways? Although research has, and indeed should, examine the questions of actual versus subjectively perceived growth, the discussion need not stop there. It is important to remember that myth has functional utility and purpose in our narrative as human beings. From the literary perspective, one may look to Greek mythology or stories from the Hebrew Scriptures or Christian New Testament, which some people understand to be myth. Although these stories may not be absolute truth from an objective point of view in the sense that Narcissus really drowned while admiring his own reflection or that Jonah was actually swallowed by a whale and lived inside the belly of the mammal, these myths are far from being nonessential to the development of individuals, communities, societies, and even our modern world. From the psychological perspective, in the quest to detangle illusion, a review of cognitive adaptation after stress and trauma reveals that not all illusion is necessarily bad. In fact, some illusions may be vitally important to trauma survivors as they attempt to reclaim their security, trust in others, and believe in their worthiness. Two theories that provide insight into understanding the function of illusions as they relate to growth will be explored: Temporal Comparison Theory and the Cognitive Adaption Theory.

Temporal Comparison Theory

In 1977, Stuart Albert of the University of Pennsylvania published a paper on temporal comparison theory that asked two important questions: (1) Is an individual who compares himself at two different points in time able to judge himself accurately? and (2) If not, does he tend to look at himself as being stronger or weaker in retrospect than he actually was?

Temporal Comparison Theory is based on the work of Festinger's (1954) social comparison theory, which examined the interpersonal comparisons that people make about each other. Festinger hypothesized that people tend to make "upward" comparisons in interpersonal relationships. That is to say that they compare themselves with others who are doing better than they are currently doing, rather than comparing themselves with others who are doing worse than they are currently doing (Taylor, 1983). Albert suggested that the same concept would translate to intrapersonal comparisons made by individuals about themselves at two different points in time.

Albert (1977) believed that individuals who are asked to recollect about themselves at two points in time will consider themselves weaker at the prior point in time and stronger at the current point of self-reflection. He supposed that individuals tend to make self-evaluations that are both inaccurate and biased because of a need individuals have to maintain an internal consistency and continuity in regard to the identity of the self. Inaccurate and biased assessments increase a person's present sense of personal well-being, because people have a tendency to believe that currently they are experiencing themselves in a better state.

Temporal Comparison Theory has applications to the discussion of the potential illusionary nature of growth. In times of trauma, temporal comparisons may be quite common. Trauma is an experience that creates a division in a person's life narrative. There is a person's life pretrauma and there is a person's life posttrauma. Temporal comparisons of self-identity pre- and posttrauma may be considered by survivors. Crisis then may be understood as an experience that initiates a process by which people confirm any differences in identity pre- and postcrisis. Following Albert's reasoning, differences found in a person's postcrisis self could be the result of a person distorting the past more negatively so that the posttrauma self can be viewed as more valuable and improved (Sumalla et al., 2009). In this way, the nature of the inaccurate representation of the past self is considered to be functional in that it may allow people to maintain a sense of internal consistency and a sense of continuity of themselves and as such increased levels of well-being. Evidence of such a theory would provide support that measures of posttraumatic growth alone may not be sufficient to demonstrate actual positive change.

Cognitive Adaption Theory

A second theory that speaks to the functional nature of illusions specifically as it relates to crisis is Taylor's (1983) cognitive adaptation theory. In examining the process of coping from the experience of a threatening life event, Taylor argues that such experiences hold at stake nothing less than the integrity of a person's very sense of self. Regardless of the characteristics of the threatening event that one experienced, three themes are universally core to the adaption process posttrauma:

1. *Meaning*—The search for meaning in the experience
2. *Mastery*—An attempt to regain mastery over the event in particular and over one's life generally
3. *Self-enhancement*—An effort to enhance one's self-esteem (p. 1161)

Drawing on data from her research with cancer patients and HIV-positive patients, her theory suggests that a fundamental principle to adapting after threatening life events is the ability to form and maintain a set of positive illusions based on the three aforementioned themes (Taylor, 1983). Taylor's term "positive illusions" does not place a person's illusions in opposition to functioning. In fact, she believed that, for many individuals who experience life-threatening events, positive illusions have a protective function that encourages people toward constructive cognitions and actions. In short, positive illusions are partly responsible for helping people heal from life-threatening experiences.

In her research with cancer patients, Taylor found that while the exact thought-specific cognitions relative to a person's positive illusion varied by individual, nearly every patient attempted to find meaning by producing cognitions about control and self-enhancement. If no cause for a person's cancer was evident, then Taylor found that people tended to invent causes for cancer that helped them to maintain a belief in control over it. Contrary to Festinger's (1954) aforementioned social comparison's theory, which stated that people tend to make upward comparisons as a function of protection of the self, Taylor found that cancer patients tended to make downward comparisons. The participants in Taylor's research found self-protection by making self-evaluations in which they compared themselves with people doing worse than they currently were relative to treatment. If people did not exist in their life who were in actuality doing worse relative to treatment, Taylor found that participants made comparisons with hypothetical individuals. Such downward comparisons then served a functional adaptive nature in the lives of the participants.

Taylor's research argues that positive illusions, such as those evidenced in her research, are critical to a person's sense of mental health and necessary for one's adjustment after threatening life events. The presence of these positive illusions allows people to return to baseline levels of functioning posttrauma and helps some people to even move beyond such levels of functioning (what the literature now refers to as growth). Taylor wrote:

> In our own work, it is clear that the sense of meaning, mastery, and self-enhancement, and the specific cognitions through which they are achieved, enable people to make sense of the cancer, to take control in aspects of themselves and their lives in ways that are self-enhancing and psychologically beneficial. The effective individual in the face of threat, then, seems to be one who permits the development of illusions, nurtures those illusions, and is ultimately restored by those illusions. (p. 1168)

The work of Janoff-Bulman (1992), which cites the work of Taylor (1983), speaks of a related concept relative to the fundamental themes of processing trauma. Janoff-Bulman argues that the core assumptions from which we operate, which she cites as *meaningfulness*, *benevolence*, and *self-esteem*, are in actuality overgeneralizations, and as such a sort of illusion. It is very easy to find examples that speak to how the world is not always meaningful or benevolent; how individuals are not always regarded in high-esteem. However, Janoff-Bulman argues that to some degree such overgeneralizations are necessary for healthy functioning. This becomes especially evident for a person who has experienced extreme stress or trauma.

The readoption of overgeneralizations, or positive illusions, relative to meaning, benevolence, and self-esteem, are necessary in order for trauma victims to function with health. It is necessary that they rebuild their global assumptions relative to the three aforementioned themes, even if they are partly illusions. Without these three global assumptions intact, one cannot operate in the world in healthy ways. One need not be ignorant or overly rosy about the pretrauma world, but neither can one live the dark, destructive existence of an immediate posttrauma world if one seeks mental health. Illusions allow a person to move beyond the abject darkness of a posttrauma world by allowing a certain amount of distance from the event, which in turn provides a sense of self-protection both at the initial onset and throughout the process of integrating the event (Taylor, 1983). This being said, it is important to note as well that for positive illusions to be adaptive in the coping process, they must also be coupled with an approachment of the event. Relying solely on illusions will not lead a person toward healthy functioning.

This dance—moving closer and farther away from the reexperience of the event as part of the integration process—is necessary for posttrauma adaptive coping. Adaptive illusions are more apt to serve the function of avoidance, which is needed in the integration process, whereas maladaptive illusions are more likely to serve the function of denial. Avoidance acknowledges the reality of an event and a natural desire to maintain distance, because of its known painful characteristics, whereas denial is a refusal to acknowledge the event for what it is, thus moving a person farther away from the ultimate goal of integration.

Clinically, and in regard to the research studies that guide our clinical interventions, it is necessary to flesh out the extent to which illusions function as a means of avoidance and when they function as a means of denial. Researchers have just started to examine such important distinctions in posttraumatic growth research, though as clinicians, we are sometimes able to hear the difference in the narrative of the client whose only experience is of denial and the narrative of the trauma victim who is engaged in the dance between avoidance and approachment as a means of self-protection in their journey toward adaptive processing and full integration.

Take, for example, Mark, a 21-year-old college senior who was out with his friends on a Friday night at a bar not too far off campus. After spending time at the bar socializing with friends, he and two friends left the bar and started walking the short distance back to their shared apartment. Within minutes of leaving the bar, a car pulled up next to the threesome and, in what appeared to be targeted fashion, someone in the car shot one of Mark's friends at very close range and repeatedly. His friend immediately fell to the ground. Mark reported that he made no movements and was not breathing. When paramedics responded to the scene, Mark's friend, who also happened to be his roommate for the first 2 years of college, was pronounced dead. It was the first time that Mark had witnessed a death, and beyond this it was the first person close to Mark to die.

When he was approached by several people immediately after the event as well as months after the event, Mark denied that the experience was affecting him in any way. In fact, it was not until many weeks into therapy that Mark even mentioned witnessing the traumatic event. When Mark presented for therapy many months after the event, his grades had markedly decreased and his alcohol consumption had markedly increased. He was having trouble sleeping. His appetite had diminished. When asked about the event, Mark indicated, "There is not much to say. I've come to the conclusion that that is what God wanted to happen, and so I just moved on." It was clear from Mark's responses that he was not engaged in any cognitive dance. Mark's global assumptions of the meaningfulness of the event as an act of God were not functioning to help him integrate the traumatic experience. This is not to say that spirituality and religion always serve the function of maladaptive denial, but in Mark's case, a global assumption that God meant for his friend to die was merely allowing him to avoid any processing and integration of the event.

When working with clients who may be experiencing denial, we must remember that denial must be worked through in order to experience integration and potential growth. However, identification of denial can be honored as a promising step in the clinical process that may allow the therapist insight into a client's ability to integrate stress and trauma. Neimeyer, Keesee, and Fortner (2000), researchers of the relationship between grief and meaning, suggest:

> *Denial* is understood as an individual's inability to assimilate a death event at a given time. One does not have recourse to the structure necessary to fully perceive the loss or its implications for one's continued living. Denial therefore represents an attempt to "suspend" the unassimilable event for a time, until its meaning can be grasped in all of its painful clarity. (p. 208)

The Janus Face Model of Self-Perceived Posttraumatic Growth

In the discernment between illusion and truth there is the possibility of a different, more complex understanding that would not put growth exclusively into either categorical box. For it is also possible that growth includes *both* components. In fact, evidence is starting to accumulate that speaks to just that possibility.

Although some researchers question whether growth is either entirely illusion or reality (basing their work on theories of adaptation relative to trauma that have existed in the psychological literature for some time), others are seeking to pioneer a less extreme approach: Not denying the possibility of illusion on the one hand, nor the simultaneous possibility for the veracity of growth at the other extreme. The Janus Face model of self-perceived posttraumatic growth, which is the work of Andreas Maercker of the University of Zurich, Switzerland, and Tanja Zoellner of Dresden University of Technology in Germany (Maercker & Zoellner, 2004; Zoellner & Maercker, 2006b), is one of the approaches that seeks to find this balance.

Maercker and Zoellner understand posttraumatic growth as having two sides. The *first side* is the "constructive, self-transcending side" (Zoellner, Rabe, Karl, & Maercker, 2008, p. 246), which is conceptualized by Tedeschi and Calhoun as "posttraumatic growth (2005)," Joseph and Linley as "adversarial growth" (2005), and Park (2005b) as "stress-related growth," whereas the *second side* of posttraumatic growth represents a "deceptive, illusionary side" (Zoellner et al., 2008, p. 246) as conceptualized by Taylor (1983). The overall premise of the model is this: If the growth that is experienced is actual, then theoretically with time, the illusionary side of growth should decrease as a person needs the positive illusions less as one moves toward integration of the event. In addition, actual growth should increase as one comes to understand the self and his or her world during the postintegration of trauma phase.

Maercker and Zoellner do not suppose that illusions are fundamentally bad or good. Rather, they explore the nature and function of illusions, understanding that not all illusions serve the same function. The usefulness of an illusion depends on the extent to which it allows a person to cognitively engage in maladaptive coping strategies (such as denial) versus the extent to which it allows a person to cognitively engage in adaptive coping strategies (Maercker & Zoellner, 2004). Such distinction is determined by three factors:

1. The timing of the coping process
2. One's individual level of psychological distress
3. One's habitual coping styles, openness to experience, or optimism (Maercker & Zoellner, 2004)

Maercker and Zoellner's theory of a two-component model highlights the conflicting data that exists in the empirical literature around the significance of the relationship between posttraumatic growth and both psychological well-being and adjustment. Some studies find relationships with such aspects of well-being as positive affect (Abraido-Lanza, Guier, & Colon, 1998; Helgeson et al., 2006; Linley & Joseph, 2004; Park et al., 1996), but other studies do not (Salsman et al., 2009). (See further discussion of this in Chapter 5 on positive emotions and growth.) Maercker and Zoellner (2004) argue that the reason for the conflicting results may be that actual posttraumatic growth may be correlated to mental health, whereas *perceived* growth may not, because in the end it is self-deception and, as such, is a distortion.

Preliminary research supportive of the two-sided model comes from a sample of former political prisoners captured from East Germany before the destruction of the Berlin wall (Maercker, 1998; Maercker & Zoellner, 2004). In the sample, quantitative and qualitative methods were used to assess the veracity of growth. Evidence was found that indicated individuals who reported personal growth tended to report one of two different coping strategies: (1) coping that signified constructive reappraisal representative of actual growth, or (2) coping that signified distractive palliation representative of illusionary forms of growth.

Maercker and Zoellner suggest in their own words:

> If a person tries solely to look at the bright side of life while denying the negative consequences of the trauma and is reluctant to deal with its impact, the self-perception of post-traumatic growth may turn into a form of cognitive avoidance with negative effects on adjustment. . . . If, however, the illusory component of posttraumatic growth does not hinder the individual from acknowledging his or her distress and the negative consequences of the trauma and does not hold back the individual from cognitive processing (but just helps to make the struggle a bit more bearable), then there should be no long-term effect of the illusory component of posttraumatic growth on adjustment. (Maercker & Zoellner, 2004, p. 47)

Research on the Question of the Veracity of Growth

Beyond the work of Maercker and Zoellner, several studies have explicitly examined the relationship between "perceived growth" and "actual growth" of an individual. Many of the studies are longitudinal, following participants over at least two points in time (Gunty et al., 2011; Ransom et al., 2008; Wolchik, Coxe, Tein, Sandler, & Ayers, 2008–2009). Some studies that attempt to assess the veracity of growth use matched comparison group designs (Gunty et al., 2011; Frazier & Kaler, 2006). Additionally, some studies use other means for examining the veracity of growth scores in cross-sectional (one point in time) studies (Park et al., 1996; Salsman et al., 2009). Taken together, the studies, along with current thinking on adaptive and maladaptive coping, suggest that there may very well be a perceived/illusionary side to growth along with an accurate/veridical side. With this data, the implications for clinical work become interesting and a bit more complex.

Frazier et al. (2009) examined a sample of 122 undergraduate students both pre- and posttrauma. The students were followed for a 2-month period. Participants completed measures of posttraumatic growth pre- and posttrauma event. Actual growth changes (as measured by differences between pre- and posttrauma) were compared to perceived growth (the measure of growth posttrauma) for those participants who experienced and reported a stressful or traumatic event during the 2 months. Researchers in the study found only a small relationship existed between perceived and actual growth. The posttraumatic growth scores were related to higher levels of distress and positive reappraisal forms of coping. The study suggests that the growth scores posttrauma, or what had been conceived as growth, may be merely a form of coping and not growth as indicated as a process outlined by Tedeschi and Calhoun (2005).

However, the results cannot be understood outside of the limitations of the study. With this in mind, one may wonder if 2 months is an adequate duration of time for the process of posttraumatic growth to occur. Additionally, when a lower-than-expected relationship between any two variables is evidenced, as was the case in the study between actual and perceived growth, one is left to wonder if moderator variables may be at play (Gunty et al., 2011), or variables whose presence are a condition of the relationship between perceived and actual growth.

To that end, Gunty et al. (2011) examined potential moderators of the relationship between perceived and actual growth in a sample of 244 undergraduates in a matched comparison, longitudinal study design. A total of 122 students who reportedly experienced a trauma were matched with 122 students who reportedly had not experienced a trauma and evaluated them over the course of 2 months. Results of the study indicated that in the trauma group, there was a significantly stronger association between perceived and actual growth for individuals who also experienced decreased levels of distress and greater satisfaction with life not evidenced in the nontrauma matched group. The results suggest that the Post-traumatic Growth Inventory may reflect actual growth experiences for some people, under certain conditions. The study suggests that accurate results may be possible to obtain from people posttrauma who experience low distress and high satisfaction with life. Other conditional factors may have yet to be determined as well.

A study by Ransom, Sheldon, and Jacobsen (2008) also examined actual versus illusionary growth in a sample of 83 male and female adults with Stage 0 to 3 breast or prostate cancer scheduled to undergo radiation therapy. Participants completed a measure of personal attributes and a measure of intrinsic and extrinsic personal goals before radiation therapy. Approximately six weeks later, after radiation therapy, participants completed the same measures, once in regard to their current state and once to recall their pretrauma measures. Posttreatment participants also completed a measure of posttraumatic growth. Comparisons were then made between actual changes (differences between time 1 and time 2 assessments) and perceived changes (differences between time 2 and time 1 recalled assessments) in regards to both personal attributes and goal motivations of participants.

In regard to personal attributions, the results indicated that between time 1 and time 2, there was an actual change between how people rated their positive attributes such that people rated themselves more positively. The comparison of the recalled time 1 and time 2 results indicated that people perceived positive attributes as increasing over time. Finally, differences between the time 1 ratings and the time 1 recalled ratings suggested that people recalled their time 1 attributes as having been more favorable than they reported. The same comparisons of time were made in regard to the intrinsic and extrinsic goal orientation. Results suggested that participants demonstrated an actual shift toward a more intrinsic goal orientation; individuals, however, did not perceive this shift, and individuals recalled their original goal orientation as more intrinsic than it was in actuality. Results also indicated that both actual change in goal orientation and perceived change in positive attributes significantly predicted growth. Taken together, the study suggests that change captured by growth scales may in fact be in part both accurate and illusionary.

Cheng, Wong, and Tsang (2006) provide further evidence for a two-component model of growth. Data from their 18-month longitudinal study in Hong Kong after the severe acute respiratory syndrome (SARS) epidemic suggests that those who gave accounts of only benefits also demonstrated being more defensive than individuals who gave accounts of *both* benefits and costs of enduring the stress and trauma related to SARS. The results suggest that exclusively finding benefits may not be healthy, and clinically an intervention may be warranted when the sole response after stress and trauma is positivity. In their words:

> If a respondent who has experienced trauma gives an exclusive account of benefits, efforts should be taken to mitigate defensiveness so as to explore and acknowledge the negative consequences of adversity. (p. 877)

While some studies have found evidence for both actual and perceived growth, other studies have evidenced only the veracity of growth. For example, Wolchik et al. (2008–2009) also used a longitudinal study design to examine the veracity of posttraumatic growth in a sample of 50 parentally bereaved adolescents and young adults over a period of 6 years. Results provide evidence of the temporal precedence of the factors that have been hypothesized to be associated with growth existing before the existence of growth. Specifically, active coping, social support from parents/guardians, and internalizing and externalizing problems measured at the start of the study predicted experiences of posttraumatic growth assessed 6 years later. Such data strengthens any arguments made for temporal precedence as one of the necessary conditions for the causal relationship examined (Wolchik et al., 2008–2009).

Several other studies also provide further evidence for the veracity of posttraumatic growth in different ways. For instance, Park et al. (1996) provides supportive evidence by demonstrating that research participants' subjective measures of posttraumatic growth were corroborated with observer ratings of growth. As well, Weiss (2004), in a study of married couples in which the wife was diagnosed with breast cancer, found that patients' posttraumatic growth scores predicted their husbands' posttraumatic growth scores. Furthermore, Salsman et al. (2009), in a sample of 55 posttreatment colorectal cancer survivors, found that posttraumatic growth did not correlate with a measure of social desirability.

Overall, the data available on assessing the truth or myth of growth seems to be supportive that posttraumatic growth measures may be able to accurately capture the theoretical process conceptualized in posttraumatic growth. However, for some individuals, scales may capture both actual growth and aspects that are perceived but not actual. In part this may happen because individuals may have a difficult time assessing intrapersonal changes (Neisser, 1994). Actual and perceived changes may be captured in measurements of growth because of the functional need people have to overgeneralize their assumptions posttrauma (Janoff-Bulman, 1992; Taylor, 1983). Still for others, scales may not capture actual growth because the individual completing the measure may be engaging in a maladaptive process such as the sole use of denial posttrauma to avoid the coping process (Gunty et al., 2011).

Results from the various studies paint a complex picture of the ability to accurately measure growth and the care that is needed both in research and clinically, when assessing for growth experiences posttrauma. However, the complexity of the research, which captures the complexity of human experience posttrauma, should not disuade the clinician from the evidence that supports aspects of growth that appear to be very real.

Clinical Implications of Assessing the Veracity of Growth

It is important from an empirical frame that we move closer to understanding the intricacies and complexities of the process leading to true posttraumatic growth. The aim of empirical research is to bring us closer to that understanding. To this end, researchers attempt to understand actual, as opposed to perceived, growth. Beyond assessing actual growth, researchers seek to understand what function the different forms of growth may play in people's lives as they navigate their posttrauma world. Although such research questions are meritorious in their own right, these questions carry important clinical implications as well—not only for the answers that may follow, but also for the implications related to merely asking the questions. With this in mind, as clinicians, we must wonder how the pursuit of understanding the veracity of growth affects the work we do with our clients.

At this point, it seems there are at least five ways that the search for understanding the veracity of growth may affect the work we do clinically. First, while it may certainly be incorrect to assume that all change reported in research studies and in clinical settings is objective change (Park, 2009), the idea of assessing the veracity of growth holds implicitly with it the risk that we as clinicians may forsake our role as therapist and guide for the role of the truth-seeker. With knowledge that growth has two sides, we may become fixated on whether our client is experiencing real growth or not. Although it is very clinically useful to have a curious stance as a therapist (Boy & Pine, 1999), the role of truth-seeker may not be a very clinically useful role at times.

As Sommers-Flanagan and Sommers-Flanagan (2009) remind us in their book on clinical interviewing, our role is not one of judge but of therapist: "It is not our job to judge whether or not someone is telling the truth, but it is our job to help people tell their story" (p. 321). Accordingly, if clinicians become too preoccupied with being certain that the growth someone is experiencing is truly real (which is something we cannot absolutely achieve anyway), then they run the risk of not involving themselves in the work that they can and should be doing. For instance, clinicians need to help clients flesh out the ways in which a new understanding of themselves, others, or the world is taking shape in their cognitions, emotions, and being in life. This is obviously important, because through the process of examining new perspectives, clinicians improve the chances of greater clarity as to whether the perceived growth is merely denial or if it is facilitating greater health in the client. Tedeschi and Calhoun (1995) remind us:

> Clinicians need to develop an increased tolerance for the individual tendency to perceive benefits from suffering, even if from the clinician's point of view this involves a certain degree of illusion. . . So when an individual sees what he or she believes to be a benefit arising from misfortune, professionals committed to the "truth" should guard against the temptation of robbing that individual of the freedom to view life's events from his or her own perspective. (p. 101)

A second important point to hold in our minds when considering the clinical application of the veracity of growth is the remembrance that much more of our reality is construed by us than we often acknowledge. From Buddhist psychology we understand that much of what we believe as a real self (an ego) can be understood as illusion: what we believe about ourselves; what we hold to as secure; what we believe is permanent in our lives. The process of self-reflection toward greater personal awareness becomes possible when we examine our self-illusions through therapy. From this perspective, it is less important that the therapist grasp the illusion than it is for clients to make the distinction. Our role is to be non-judgmental as they come to see themselves by distinguishing the illusions and the reality. Like the research literature on the veracity of growth, the teachings of Buddhist psychology also note the connections between change and illusion and highlight in particular how part of real change, even when the change is positive, can invoke fear. The knowledge of the relationship between fear and the process of change can inform our work in that we can help clients find strategies to meet fear and to explore their relationship with change. As Unno notes: "Part of us wants to change, part of us is deeply frightened at the prospect of changing and will often settle for the illusion instead of the real thing" (Unno, 2006, p. 18).

The third important clinical implication is held in acknowledging the paradoxical nature of illusions and what that means when sitting with clients. As we saw in this chapter, illusions at their heart may contain elements of both adaptive coping and maladaptive forms of coping. So then to work effectively with clients, we must frame the awareness of both ways of coping (i.e., avoidance and denial) as potentially useful clinically. When we hold a wish to remove aspects of a person (e.g., their denial), we are no longer working with the person; instead, we are working with who we want the person to become. Our work as counselors is to be present with the whole client in the now, as fragmented as he or she may be. To do this, it may be helpful to keep in mind that growth may be effective in a person's search for well-being even if it is merely perception (Park, 2009).

Fourth, with the information that is provided, and with each of the previous understandings held in mind, we can hopefully then better serve our clients in that we can hold a general awareness that not all signs of growth are intrinsically good in all clients. In the end, clients are individuals, and the way they experience and use forms of growth may certainly be functional and adaptive in one person and lack those qualities in another. It is abundantly clear that at the heart of clinical work it is not the statistics (though this can be very helpful in our work in many ways) or ratios of what is real (versus what is not), but our efforts to understand the cognitions, sentiments, and experiences that our clients hold. We are implored to know the how, what, and way that they hold such things and the relationship that each has with their sense of well-being.

Lastly, and most importantly, the clinical implications of the research on the veracity of growth remind us of how deeply important the concept of truth is in trauma work. To tell the truth and to have truth is integral to the healing process. We do not need to be truth-seekers, but we need to be truth believers. We must hold this as a core and present stance that encourages a desire to bear witness to the expression of truth. For to be successful as a therapist necessitates a belief that the truth-telling will ultimately set a person, community, and a world, captured by traumatic events, free.

A Quote to Remember

It is not our job to judge whether or not someone is telling the truth, but it is our job to help people tell their story (Sommers-Flanagan & Sommers-Flanagan, 2009, p. 321).

Clinical Cornerstones of the Chapter

- Illusions may be positive in that they help people regain new global assumptions after traumatic experiences. They are the bridges to a new land of meaning and living for them that may even surpass in some ways how they have viewed the world and lived in the past.
- Clinically, it is necessary to distinguish the extent to which illusions are used as a means of avoidance or denial. A way to accomplish this is by appreciating together the fruits of the tentative myth being offered.
- We are sometimes able to hear the difference in the narrative of the client whose only experience is of denial as opposed to

the narrative of trauma victims who are engaged in the dance between avoidance and approachment. In the latter instance, it is a means of self-protection in their journey toward adaptive processing and full integration.

• Much more of our reality is construed by us than we often acknowledge. As we know with all of our clients as well as with our own life: Perception is the powerful window we look through that can make a hell of heaven or a heaven of hell.

• "Part of us wants to change, part of us is deeply frightened at the prospect of changing, and we will often settle for the illusion instead of the real thing" (Unno, 2006, p. 18). Is the illusion like a menu before having a good meal, or is it a defensive alternative and avoidance to living a better life? That is the question.

• If a respondent who has experienced trauma gives an exclusive account of benefits it offers, efforts should be taken to mitigate defensiveness so as to explore and acknowledge the negative consequences of adversity as well (Cheng et al., 2006, p. 877). Progress often depends on eventually embracing a balanced picture of the experience.

Selected References

Maercker, A., & Zoellner, T. (2004). The Janus Face of self-perceived growth: Toward a two-component model of posttraumatic growth. *Psychological Inquiry, 15,* 41–48.
This research article presents a model of posttraumatic growth that includes self-perceived growth both as illusion and as actual growth.

Ransom, S., Sheldon, K. M., & Jacobsen, P. B. (2008). Actual change and inaccurate recall contribute to posttraumatic growth following radiotherapy. *Journal of Consulting and Clinical Psychology, 76,* 811–819.

This research article provides statistical evidence of both perceived and actual growth.

Taylor, S. E. (1983). Adjustment to threatening events. A theory of cognitive adaptation. *American Psychologist, 38,* 1161–1173.

This article is the primary text for cognitive adaptation theory presented by Shelley Taylor. Her work in the area of cognitive adaption theory is heavily cited by Janoff-Bulman in her work on trauma, *Shattered Assumptions* (1992). This article provides detailed information on the ways in which cognitive adaptations in regard to our search for meaning, our attempts to regain mastery, and our movements toward reclaiming self-esteem after threatening events in part necessitate functional illusions.

Wolchik, S. A., Coxe, S., Tein, J. Y., Sandler, I. N., & Ayers, T. S. (2008–2009). Six-year longitudinal predictors of posttraumatic growth in parentally bereaved adolescents and young adults. *Omega: Journal of Death and Dying, 58,* 107–128.

This article provides research evidence to support the concept of posttraumatic growth as actual and not illusion.

CHAPTER 3

MEANING

All people are called at different points in their lives to psychologically lean back and reflect on how they are making sense of their lives and the world around them. Developmentally, this is obviously part of the process referred to as *maturation*. The process is also initiated when one encounters significant personal and environmental change or trauma. Whatever the circumstances though, so many potential positive psychological results are related to this search for meaning that it may even be construed as being of great import on the overall search for mental health. Meaning has been associated in the psychological literature with decreased depression, increased hope (Ai et al., 2005), increased life satisfaction, increased self-esteem (Steger & Frazier, 2005), and overall increased general and emotional health (Park & Blumberg, 2002). In essence, when we have meaning in our lives, we feel good.

What gives people meaning in their lives is as unique as each of us. In fact, when it comes to meaning—perhaps like no other psychological construct demands—the experience must be personal. However, there are trends in the research on how one develops new meaning to help clinicians who work with clients in this essential process. Themes stress the importance of finding meaning in such areas as relationships, work, school, spiritual, religious, or political beliefs, and the pursuit of both tangible and intangible life goals (Debats, 1999).

The concept of meaning is a distinctly human phenomenon (Baumeister & Vohs, 2002). For *homo sapiens* ("the thinking person"), meaning is one of life's basic motivations (Frankl, 1969).

As the Latin root of the word *motivation* indicates, meaning is something that *moves* us. Meaning assists in both behavioral and affect self-regulation, as well as helps us in fulfilling our needs for purpose, value, self-efficacy, and self-worth. In addition, it also allows us to better predict and control our personal and social environments (Baumeister, 1991). When we have meaning, we have a "why." And as the philosopher Nietzsche reminds us, "He who has a *why*, can endure any *how*."

In life—and more understandably in therapy—the presence and the process of meaning-making can be done formally, informally, or at times without any serious reflection. Although people do not always acknowledge the presence and import of meaning in their lives, they can be painfully aware when it is missing. Clients may not express directly that their concerns come from a lack of being able to find meaning in life. Instead, terms may be used that in essence describe the experience that results from a lack of meaning. Clients may use terms such as "bad," "empty," "uneasy," or "lost." Therefore, a therapist would do well to keep such terms in mind as indicators that a person's goal of meaning-making may be going, or have already gone, awry. Perhaps the most evident clinical signal that meaning may be of concern is the expression of a considerable sense of distress, which accompanies, and even initiates, a search for meaning (Yalom, 1980). Additionally, such distress may actually be what moves a client to seek therapy in the first place.

Sadly, such distress that drives a person to undertake a search for meaning may feel as though it is all too much to bear for some clients if therapeutic intervention is not sought or provided correctly. When a client presents with distress surrounding meaning, it must be taken quite seriously and attended to with great care.

Take for example the words written by Mitchell Heisman, a 35-year-old man who committed suicide in September 2010. In a

1,905-page suicide note that Heisman left behind, his expressed fundamental concern pointed to an overwhelming inability to successfully find meaning in life. He wrote, "Every word, every thought, and every emotion came back to one core problem: Life is meaningless" (www.boston.com/news/local/ massachusetts/ articles/2010/09/27/book_details_motives_for_suicide_at_harvard). The words of Heisman are a painful reminder that meaning (which is sometimes even underworked or overlooked by well-meaning clinicians) is of the utmost importance. It can literally mean the difference between life and death.

After experiences of stress and trauma, meaning is of the utmost importance. In fact, meaning is a concept that very well may consciously seem to lack any relevance in a person's life until an experience of crisis occurs (Frankl, 1969). Yet, once a person experiences a crisis, the search for meaning—whether or not it is clearly acknowledged as such—usually becomes particularly important, as the research explains.

For example, a study of adults who experienced the death of a family member as a result of illness (cancer, AIDs, or cardiovascular disease) found that those family members who were able to somehow find meaning in the loss 6 months post-bereavement experienced significantly less distress than family members who were unsuccessful in making sense of their loss (Davis, Nolen-Hoeksema, & Larson, 1998). One reason why finding meaning after loss may lower levels of distress is that meaning may decrease a person's fears of recurring trauma, as was noted by a longitudinal study of the 9/11 terrorist attacks (Updergaff, Silver, & Holman, 2008). Consequently, looking at the whole process of meaning-making as a way to conceptualize clinical work with all clients—especially those who have encountered great change or trauma in their lives—can be a very helpful undertaking. One such meaning-making model of coping formulated by Park outlines the ways *new* meaning may be developed as a result of coping with stress and trauma. This idea is particularly relevant, as it has been noted that:

> The evidence to date suggests that when trauma throws into question the explicit or implicit meaning of life that a person has developed, the event may be perceived as meaningful to the extent that it provokes the development of new meanings. (Tedeschi & Calhoun, 1995, p. 75)

Park's Meaning-Making Model of Coping

In Park's meaning-making model of coping, a framework for understanding why people might engage in the search for meaning, and specifically new meaning, after experiencing a stressful or traumatic event is provided. The model, which may also prove helpful for use with other therapeutic challenges, draws theoretically on two works. First, she relies on the work of Frankl (1969) and the premise contained in his classic work *The Will to Meaning*. In that book, written following his experiences and observations at a Nazi concentration camp, he explains that meaning is a primary motive and something that must be found to survive traumatic experiences. Without the ability to find meaning, survival of such horrific experiences may not be possible. The meaning that a person must find is not something that anyone can give to the person seeking meaning, be the person a family member, friend, or therapist. Responsibility for meaning lies in the individual who seeks it. In Frankl's (1969) words, "And meaning is something to be found, rather than to be given, discovered rather than invented" (p. 62).

Secondly, Park's theory draws upon, and is a development of, the transactional theory of emotion and coping (Lazarus & Folkman, 1987), which examines the cognitive appraisals that people make during stressful events and the potential coping strategies that can follow such appraisals (Park, 2005a; see Lazarus & Folkman, 1987 for further detail).

Park's meaning-making model states that when a person experiences traumatic life events, the traditional models of coping (problem-focused or emotion-focused) are not very productive because trauma is not "solvable" or "repairable" (Park, 2005a). Therefore, the coping process following extreme stress and trauma must be necessarily different in nature than traditional methods. Accordingly, she states that coping with such life experiences necessitates the involvement of a more intrapsychic cognitive process that Park calls "meaning-making." Although this process through the years has referred to many things, for Park it specifically points to the tenet that only through a *cognitive adaptation* can a person come to transform intensely stressful life experiences (Park, 2005a). Further examination of this model explains why she believes this to be so and merits attention here.

There are two forms of meaning articulated by Park's meaning-making model. The first, *global meaning*, describes an overall view or interpretation of life. Global meaning consists of a:

- Series of beliefs about the world and self (in regard to justice, fairness, control, and predictability)
- Series of goals often aimed at maintaining equilibrium of current objects or states (Klinger, 1998)
- Subjective sense of meaningfulness that comes from a level of awareness that one's behaviors are leading toward a desired state or goal (Park, 2005a)

Global meaning translates into daily meaning by influencing interpretations of the world around the person. Global goals influence daily strivings and projects. Finally, a subjective sense of meaningfulness influences feelings of life satisfaction and positive affect (Park, 2005a). The second form of meaning, *situational meaning*, on the other hand, as the name presumes, is that which is assigned to *specific* life events (Park & Folkman, 1997). In times of stress and trauma, situational meaning references the meaning that one assigns to the stressful or traumatic event.

The difference in the two belief systems becomes important when a person undergoes a significant stressor, such as trauma. Trauma can threaten or shatter an individual's assumptive world (Janoff-Bulman, 1992)—the very standard against which the self and life is interpreted (Matthews & Marwit, 2006). When this happens, a conflict between belief systems may result. For example, one may operate with a global belief that the world is safe. If the person then undergoes a traumatic experience (e.g., being abused), this requires that he or she assigns a new situational belief that the world was not safe in this instance.

The goal of one's belief systems is to remain balanced. Therefore, the discrepancies in belief systems result in distress. This negative experience of feeling distress then initiates a new meaning-making process to restore violated or disrupted global meaning and to reestablish once-violated assumptions in order to restore feelings of control and predictability as a way of decreasing distress. How effective such a process is will go a long way toward decreasing the distress that living with such an inner discrepancy may produce.

Park and Blumberg (2002) found that the desired balance between belief systems can be restored through a reappraisal process commonly referred to as cognitive processing. One reappraisal process involves altering the situational meaning assigned to the event. This occurs by assimilating the trauma into previously held global beliefs. No new meaning is made, but rather people are able to integrate the event into their previous understandings of themselves and the world. Another reappraisal process involves the altering of global beliefs to accommodate the possibility of the event. The accommodation of global beliefs can be either in the positive or negative direction. Take, for example, a woman who is the victim of a sexual assault who before the assault held a global assumption that the world was safe. If she accommodates her situational experience in a negative direction, she may form a new global belief that the world is unsafe and no one is to be trusted. However, if she accommodates her situational experience in a positive way, she may come to believe new things about herself such as she is a stronger person than she thought she was before the trauma, or hold a new belief that she can handle many more life experiences than she ever thought she could before the event.

If the cognitive processing changes a person's situational or global beliefs such that there is no longer a conflict or drastic disparity between the two forms of meanings, then a person no longer feels distress, and the meaning-making process ends. However, if the new meaning doesn't harmonize the person's two levels of meaning, then the individual continues to cycle through the meaning-making process until the two levels of beliefs are congruent (Park, 2005a).

As has been articulated in the research on meaning and loss, there are many different ways to define meaning-making (Davis et al., 2000). An important notation here in regard to the meaning-making model of coping is that meaning-making, in the context that Park describes it, does not mean that people necessarily understand on the deepest level that they wanted an event to happen in their life even if it has produced good outcomes such as having a greater appreciation for the gift of life and deeper compassion for others—this is especially the case with people suffering the pain of trauma. Rather, it simply signifies that something *new* is understood (e.g., new meaning is made).

Park and Blumberg (2002) tested the meaning-making process by examining the extent to which writing about a traumatic event was associated with reappraisals in situational meaning and global beliefs or goals in a sample of 157 male and female college students. The study was an experimental design in which students were randomly assigned to either a trauma writing group or a control group. The students were given 4 days of writing assignments. Significant differences were found between the trauma writing group and the control group between day 1 and day 4 based on scores related to measures of general and emotional health, stress appraisal, and meaning. Students in the trauma writing group increased on all measures. The results suggest that writing about trauma facilitated the meaning-making process, as evidenced by participants in the writing group's decrease in adverse appraisals of situational meaning and in cognitive processing.

A 4-month follow-up study by the same authors found that changes were stable over time. The authors also examined a third experimental group in which students were asked to identify, but not write about, a traumatic event. Results indicated no change on meaning scales, providing evidence for the meaning-making model of coping and suggesting that meaning-making is a process that requires deliberate—possibly repeated—reflection. For the clinician, this is important because it suggests the usefulness that providing narrative structure (through talking and writing about a traumatic events) can offer to a person's experience of well-being following loss.

Posttraumatic Growth as a Result of Meaning-Making

Park's (2005a) model then is a useful way of understanding how meaning-making can result in the experience of positive changes that follow stressful life events. One way growth is thought to result from meaning is related to repeated exposures and attempts to work through the stress and trauma that are part of the meaning-making process. People do not necessarily move through the process in a linear fashion. Additionally, discrepancies in meaning are rarely restored on the first try. Rather, people usually repeatedly cycle through the process until the discrepancy between meaning systems is resolved. This drawn-out process is not necessarily a drawback in that it is thought that such repeated exposure to working through the event may also aid people in creating a more integrated understanding of the stressful and traumatic event. This, in turn, may then help the person to identify previously unforeseen redeeming features of the event, which can improve their future adaptation to challenge and change, as well as improve their quality of life (Park & Ai, 2006, Tedeschi & Calhoun, 2004).

The research evidence for posttraumatic growth as a result of the meaning-making model is strong and continues to accumulate (Park, 2008). For instance, in one study, a sample of 108 male and female college students who experienced a major loss primarily within 6 months before the study completed measures of global and situational beliefs, coping, distress, and stress-related growth in a repeated measures study over a 6-week period. Results indicated that:

- People who experience significant loss also experience discrepancies between global beliefs or goals and appraised meaning of loss (e.g., a global belief that a mother will always be present as a mentor and guide and the appraised meaning of a mother's death as abandonment).
- Perceived loss as a violation of global meaning is associated with more distress.
- More perceived discrepancies are related to less positive affect, more negative affect, more depressive symptoms, and less posttraumatic growth (Park, 2008).

A second way of understanding growth that may follow the meaning-making process (Neimeyer, 2006) indicates that as people attempt to decrease discrepancies among their previously held beliefs, they may assimilate the information of the stress or trauma into their preexisting global assumptions in a way that affirms their beliefs in different ways. This affirmation of beliefs lends itself to the possibility of growth experiences. For example, if a relative dies and a person had a certain image of God, how that person comes to terms with this previously held image may be affirmed by the death in a different way, or this former image of God may change in ways that aid in providing future increased resiliency and increased enjoyment of one's life.

Take, for example, Ben, a 22-year-old recent college graduate whose brother died tragically in a climbing accident months after Ben's graduation. Before the death of his brother, Ben held an image of God as someone who was only part of Sunday church services. God was a distant figure who existed in a box that he only opened on Sundays for an hour or so and then quickly closed again once church services ended. However, after the accident and his brother's death, Ben began to reexamine the image of God he held. He began to reexamine the way in which God existed in his life. He began to realize that he could access God outside of church services, and doing this was useful to him. He did not have to wait until Sunday at noon to have a conversation with God, and he did not need to wait for God to start that conversation. After the death of his brother, Ben experienced God as much closer to him than he had once believed. His God image was more present for him to access in future life stresses, allowing him to experience a sense of more joy in life, even with a more full and personal recognition of the pain that existed and continued to exist in life too.

There are two important notes for clinicians about growth following stress and trauma that become clear from the meaning-making perspective of coping. First, examination of growth following stress and trauma from a meaning-making perspective helps those who work with trauma victims to appreciate that the positive changes experienced do not come from the trauma per se but from the confrontation and struggle to cope (Tedeschi & Calhoun, 2004). This caveat is of the utmost importance when working with clients. In no way does a clinician want to ignore or trivialize the great intrapsychic pain and intrinsic negativity of stress and trauma. Second, the meaning-making perspective of stress and trauma articulates that the meaning-making cycle only ends once the discrepancies between meaning systems is restored. Therefore, in the meaning-making process of coping, *posttraumatic growth may be considered a signal of cognitive closure* (Park, Edmondson, Fenster, & Blank, 2008). Growth will then remain limited if a person is still actively involved in the search for meaning.

An additional important clinical point of the meaning-making process that is not outlined from the previous studies but that is expressed in the literature is the great importance of considering the broader social context in which a person attempts to engage in the meaning-making process, for example:

> The reconstruction of a personal world of meaning in the wake of loss must take into account our ongoing relationships with real and symbolic others. . . . To understand even the most private dimensions of loss, we must place them in a social context that supports, opposes, or ignores our experience and need to change. Conflicts or contested meanings in these social contexts contribute to difficulties in adapting to loss, whereas consonance in the multiple social circles that are affected by loss can support a more coherent revision of our life narratives. (Neimeyer et al., 2000, p. 210)

A more detailed understanding the role of social relationships and social context in relationship to posttraumatic growth specifically will be explored in Chapter 7.

Meaning-Making and Clinical Work

As can be surmised from what has been presented thus far, therapeutic relationships with those who have experienced trauma will probably necessitate a review of meaning with them at some point in the treatment. How this is done and who initiates a discussion of meaning are crucial elements in the successful inclusion into the treatment process though. Therapists must remember that finding meaning will most likely not be the number-one priority of a client who is still actively struggling with extreme distress and attempting to comprehend that the event did indeed take place (Tedeschi & Calhoun, 1995). In this light, therapists must remember that it is not they who search for positive meaning; it is the client who needs this meaning, and as such, it must come in the client's own time. However, as Tedeschi and Calhoun (1995) suggest, "The clinician can assist survivors in creating a narrative account of what has happened that makes sense and includes positive outcomes from the struggle" (p. 111). Clinicians can do this by listening for the client's search, and when positive meaning is claimed, see the signal to then discuss and honor it. This delicate discernment on the part of the clinician can have a *significant* impact on the course of treatment of persons who have experienced trauma.

There are many ways to enable or respond to the client's search for meaning; however, while a great deal of work has been done clinically and theoretically, research in regard to specific use of the techniques to facilitate posttraumatic growth via meaning-making has not been fully documented. Further research is needed before a statement of evidence-based practices in facilitating posttraumatic growth is to be claimed. Still, the empirical literature is gaining a good deal of documentation for the support of narrative therapy in work concerning meaning and trauma, especially when meaning-making is involved.

Narrative work conceptualizes trauma as a disruption of a person's life narrative (Neimeyer, 2000, 2001). People who experience trauma may respond by actively searching for some sense of meaning. Instances of trauma may force individuals to make sense of traumatic events. This reconstruction of meaning resolves the interruption and allows for narrative cohesion rather than simply a positive reframe of a tragic event (Neimeyer, 2000). Given this, as clinicians it is important to recognize more specifically that the meaning-making process may involve:

- The re-evaluation, reinterpretation, and restructuring of a person's life narrative that leads to an integration of loss
- A reappraisal of personal identity
- The ability to eventually find new meaning in one's life post-trauma (Matthews & Marwit, 2006)

Narrative therapy seeks to provide structure to a person's life story and as such can be quite powerful in the search and integration of meaning after stress and trauma (Neimeyer, 2006). Oral narrative techniques are one way to encourage narrative structure. Neimeyer (2006) provides the following example of Guidano's "movieola method" as a means for clients to find meaning and self-continuity posttrauma:

Emotionally discrepant episodes in a client's self-narrative can be "replayed" through slow-motion recall and re-narration, focusing the "camera" of therapeutic attention on particularly painful details, or "panning out" to the larger life pattern in which the problematic client was embedded. (Guidano, 1995, p. 77; see Guidano, 1995 and Neimeyer, 2006 for further information on this technique.)

Narrative structure can also be encouraged through narrative writing techniques. For example, a clinician may ask clients to write an impact statement describing how a stressful or traumatic event has impacted a person's life story. Research on victims of sexual assault has noted that continual revision of writing an impact statement can increase a client's sense of control and improve his or her own level of insight (Davis et al., 2000; Resick & Schnicke, 1992). Such an impact statement, according to narrative theory, would include a client's description of the personal meaning of the traumatic event, specifically addressing the ways in which the event has affected the way he or she has come to view the self, others, and the world (Sobel, Resick, & Rabalais, 2009).

In a similar vein, journal writing is also a way in which therapists can assist clients in finding narrative structure and encourage clients who have brought to the forefront their search for meaning after a personal tragedy. After writing, further reflection and examination of the journal writing can be done with the therapist (see Neimeyer, 2006 and Neimeyer et al., 2000 for more information on journal writing techniques).

Important Current Limitations

Sadly, although theoretical and empirical evidence suggests that the process of meaning-making is a central concern when a person experiences a stressful life event, it has also been suggested that among the groups of people at the highest risk of not finding meaning are those who experience a loss under traumatic circumstance (Davis et al., 2000). In the case of traumatic loss, the ability to find satisfactory meaning may prove for some people to be a painful, unlikely, or fruitless task (Davis et al., 2000) that leaves them continuing to feel the distress from lack of meaning associated with the stress or trauma.

Take, for example, Madeline and Alexander, who had been married for 2 years when they discovered that Madeline was pregnant. Both of them were elated. It was Madeline's first pregnancy. Alexander was able to recall and easily share numerous examples of how loving and protective Madeline was from the first moment she discovered she was to be a mother. Alexander recalled that she was perhaps overcautious with exercise, rest, and diet during her pregnancy. He shared, "She did everything right—better than right."

As is the case in many pregnancies, it was a time of great change in Madeline's life; so many changes were happening in her body that Madeline understandably assumed were all caused by pregnancy.

Alexander remembered how Madeline never complained about any of her symptoms. She was a very strong woman before pregnancy and all the way through what joyously ended with the birth of their beautiful, healthy baby girl, Ella.

A few months after delivering Ella, Madeline discovered a large lump in her right breast. At first she thought perhaps it was a clogged milk duct or another issue related to breastfeeding. She was not worried or concerned. In fact, she didn't even tell Alexander about the lump. Eventually, during a routine postpregnancy check-up, she informed her doctor about the lump, who would later diagnose the lump as Stage 3 breast cancer. Both Madeline and Alexander were in complete shock with the news.

When Madeline was diagnosed, the cancer had already spread to her lymph nodes. Still, her doctor was hopeful, and so were Madeline and Alexander for a while. However, despite hope, and despite Madeline's great inner strength, a year after her diagnosis, just shy of Ella's 15-month birthday, Madeline lost her battle with breast cancer. The death of Madeline brought Alexander great distress. He actively searched for some sort of meaning following his wife's death—immediately after it and for many years later still. He wanted more than anything to find some meaning. However, unable to do so, he eventually stopped, concluding that the experience of his wife's death was indeed completely meaningless and that he would forever live in a world of despair. When he entered therapy, almost 5 years after his wife's death, he expressed a sense of emptiness ever since Madeline died that he could not imagine would ever be filled. He was "permanently broken," he had concluded, without Madeline.

As was the case for Alexander for the 5 years after his wife's death before seeking counseling, the unfortunate paradox of the relationship between trauma and meaning is that the very group of people who may need to find meaning the most may be the least likely to do so—and not for lack of trying. Although some information is beginning to unfold in regard to the process by which people develop or restore meaning following stressful life experiences, continued research is necessary (Davis et al., 2000) so that clinicians who work with people experiencing stress and trauma can be served better.

Final Comment

No one who breathes misses the physical act of living, but everyone is at risk of living a life void of meaning. We search for meaning not like a set of lost keys that we once possessed but more like infants at night seeking proximity to their mothers. We feel her absence weaved throughout our thoughts, beliefs, and attitudes, throughout our life narratives, throughout our whole beings. We may have protection, nurturance, and even love by many other people and things in life, but we hold a sense of restlessness within. Yet, once we finally find meaning, it seems that the protection, nurturance, and love that exists in our life transforms into a way of holding us differently; with a sense of meaning in our lives we are held by people, roles, and even by certain things more honestly, deeply, and—of greatest consequence to the client who has experienced great stress and trauma in life—with a greater sense of peace within.

A Quote to Remember

In [adjustment to major losses and traumas], which are not amenable to "problem solving" strategies, coping involves a great deal of intrapsychic cognitive processes or "meaning-making," since only through cognitive adaptation can individuals transform the meaning of the stressful experience (Park, 2005a, p. 709).

Clinical Cornerstones of the Chapter

- Clinicians will find it beneficial to use narrative structure to help clients process their experiences of stress and trauma, because it can increase clients' experiences of control and their insight into events (Davis et al., 2000).

- Clinicians should listen to clients' narratives for variations between their global and situational belief systems (Fontana & Rosenheck, 2004; Park & Ai, 2006) and explore the variations, because this process is at the heart of the treatment of trauma.

- It has been suggested that among the groups of people at the highest risk of not finding meaning are those who experience a loss under traumatic circumstances (Davis et al., 2000); consequently, clinicians need to keep this awareness in mind when pacing and structuring the treatment.

- In the case of traumatic loss, the ability of individuals to find satisfactory meaning may prove to be a painful, unlikely, or even a fruitless task (Davis et al., 2000) for some people; clinical assessment is crucial in determining possibility and pacing of meaning-making interventions with clients who have been traumatized.

- We must remember that positive changes that are experienced by persons who have experienced trauma do *not* come from the trauma per se but instead from the confrontation and struggle to cope (Tedeschi & Calhoun, 2004). Therefore, great care must be taken not to ignore the significant negative impact that trauma has in people's lives as one journeys with them on their search for meaning posttrauma.

- The literature suggests that the meaning-making cycle only ends once the discrepancies between meaning systems is restored; patience and attentiveness without preconceived notions of what must happen will help balance the clinician's interventions in order to avoid either rushing the process on the one hand or underplaying the value of meaning-making on the other.

- When the meaning-making process of coping is more-or-less achieved, it is a signal of cognitive closure surrounding the event (Park et al., 2008).

- For clinicians, there needs to be a keen awareness that post-traumatic growth represents a new sense of meaning-making that helps people to realize something unique after significant darkness or trauma has occurred; namely, for the client who experiences posttraumatic growth, the sense that "I have not lost my way; I have left an old way in my world only to be greeted by a new perspective that gives me new life in sometimes greater ways here-to-fore not considered possible."
- Assumptions are shattered when a loss, trauma, or significant change takes place. However, posttrauma, a new assumptive world that offers new possibilities may be in the offing. Yet, to take advantage of this on a more permanent basis, certain steps need to be enacted in the meaning-making process that are not induced, but guided, by the clinician.

Selected References

Baumeister, R. (1991). *Meaning in life*. New York, NY: Guilford Press.
A leader in the empirical investigation of meaning in life, this book provides an overview as well as empirical evidence to support how people find meaning in life and what happens when found meaning in life is lost. Specifically addressed is the relationship between suffering and meaning.

Frankl, V. (1969). *The will to meaning: Foundations and applications of logotherapy*. New York, NY: Penguin.
Written following his experiences and observations at a Nazi concentration camp, in this book Victor Frankl explains that meaning is a primary motive and something that must be found to survive traumatic experiences. Frankl uses his experiences as a psychiatrist in the presentation of the techniques of logotherapy in practice.

Park, C. L., & Ai, A. L. (2006). Meaning-making and growth: New direction for research on survivors of trauma. *Journal of Loss and Trauma, 11,* 389–407.

An overview of the theoretical and empirical evidence to support the meaning-making model of coping relative to growth following stressful and traumatic events.

Yalom, I. (1980). *Existential psychotherapy.* New York, NY: Basic Books.

An overview of existential psychotherapy, which includes a detailed discussion on what Yalom refers to as the ultimate concern of meaninglessness.

CHAPTER 4

COGNITIVE PROCESSING

A person who has experienced a stressful or traumatic event may hold many questions posttrauma: Who or what is to blame for the stress or trauma? What could I have done to prevent the stress or trauma? What would my life have been like now if the stress or trauma had never happened? How can I live my life in this posttrauma world? A key aspect of trauma and posttraumatic growth involves cognitive processing of the stressful or traumatic experience. As was articulated in Chapter 1, traumatic events may leave a person with a shattered or fractured belief system (Janoff-Bulman, 1992)—a worldview that no longer holds true in the wake of the traumatic event. Once strongly held assumptions of how the world ought to work seem not to fit with the present reality of a world where extreme stress and trauma exist.

There is a sense of dissonance between what one's assumption of the world was and the experience of trauma that has proven to be painfully real. Discrepancies between global assumptions and traumatic events may leave a person without a guide or map to follow, which can be quite debilitating. For psychological and emotional health, people need organizational guides. The reconstruction of basic assumptions is a necessity posttrauma (Tedeschi & Calhoun, 2004). Together, a shattered belief system, the subsequent distressing feelings, a lack of comprehensibility, and lack of meaning are thought to set a person on a course of thinking about the event that may be automatic, deliberate, or both. Depending on several factors related to the way one processes the event, along with other factors, for some the process will eventually lead to posttraumatic growth (Tedeschi & Calhoun, 2004).

Repeatedly, thinking about an event is common after stress and trauma. Take, for example, the mother of a teenage girl who had very recently died of complications related to AIDS, a disease she contracted from her mother. Weeks after the incident, the mother expressed:

> I just can't stop thinking about my daughter's death. I keep thinking of that last time I saw her. I remember her trying to talk but they had a tube in her throat so she couldn't speak to me. I can't stop thinking that maybe she could not breathe. Maybe, if they had taken the tube out she would have been able to breathe better—maybe she would not have died right then. I can see the doctors standing over her. I can see all these tubes and machines. I can see her laying there, my little girl. She wasn't *supposed* to die. I am the one who was supposed to be dead. She was supposed to be alive. She was supposed to bury me. That's how life is supposed to work.

The term used to describe thinking about a stressful or traumatic event, either on purpose or, as was the case for the mother in the case example, what appears involuntary, is referred to by Tedeschi and Calhoun as *cognitive processing*. Tedeschi and Calhoun's theory draws on Martin and Tesser's (1996) conceptualization of ruminations, understanding that ruminations, while often associated only with negative content experienced automatically, are in fact not always negative or automatic. Ruminations can include positive and neutral content, along with being either intrusive or self-focused (Calhoun & Tedeschi, 1998). As is explored in this chapter, depending on the type, timing, and content of the ruminations, growth may be more possible. Additionally, ruminations, as understood by Martin and Tesser (1996), can take on a broader understanding than perhaps one may first think in that they can include the process of making sense, problem solving, reminiscing, and anticipation.

Although ruminations may often come with feelings of significant distress, and while such distress must be managed if cognitive processing is to be effective, ruminations are considered to be the very foundation on which new insights characteristic of posttraumatic growth may emerge (Calhoun & Tedeschi, 1999, Tedeschi & Calhoun, 2004). Exploration into a more complex understanding of ruminations has led researchers to understand that based on the *type*, *timing*, and *content*, ruminations are fundamental in the process of posttraumatic growth. Different forms of ruminations experienced at different times posttrauma are thought to increase the likelihood that a person will disengage from an old worldview in a potentially adaptive manner rather than a potentially maladaptive one (Calhoun & Tedeschi, 1998). Disengagement from an old worldview is essential to growth, because the more one is engaged with reclaiming a past existence that can never be in actuality reclaimed, the more distress one will experience. Additionally, the disengagement of past goals can allow for the creation of new goals that may lead a person to eventually experience positive growth (Tedeschi & Calhoun, 2004). This process of disengagement is not easy, quick, linear, or without struggle—and not experienced universally. The more that is understood about the *type*, *timing*, and *content* of ruminations, the more useful a clinician's interventions may be in facilitating growth.

Automatic and Intrusive Ruminations

There are two types of ruminations that people may have as they cognitively process stressful and traumatic experiences: *automatic* and *deliberate* ruminations. Although they are two distinct forms of ruminations, they have an important relationship in the process of posttraumatic growth.

Automatic ruminations are sometimes also referred to as intrusive ruminations. Such ruminations may include both intrusive thoughts about the traumatic event and intrusive images related to the event (Calhoun & Tedeschi, 1998; Tedeschi & Calhoun, 2004). There is a sense of a lack of control over automatic ruminations, as the name implies. Thoughts and images enter a person's mind involuntarily. When automatic ruminations are experienced, responding to them though self-disclosure either through written or verbal expression can be very beneficial. The expression of automatic ruminations, especially early on in the coping process, is thought to lead to four important results related to posttraumatic growth:

1. The reduction of emotional distress
2. The management of automatic rumination
3. Disengagement from one's previously held goals
4. Deliberate forms of rumination (Calhoun & Tedeschi, 2006, p. 8)

Several important clinical points follow the expression of automatic ruminations. First is the importance that the reduction of emotional distress has in working with clients who have experienced stress and trauma. Without the reduction of distress (which is not the same as a lack of distress), a client may not be able to engage with the content of the stress and trauma in ways that will be beneficial. Second, automatic ruminations, which by definition are experienced as happening to a person, rather than a person controlling the ruminations, should not be considered unmanageable. Although control may be experienced as being lost by the presence of intrusive thoughts and images, management of the ruminations is always possible. Third, the disengagement process of previously held goals starts with the expression of automatic ruminations, not with the expression of deliberate ruminations. Finally, there is an important relationship between automatic and deliberate forms of ruminations. Whereas automatic ruminations are not thought to lead to posttraumatic growth directly, evidence suggests that intrusive ruminations are useful in that they may lead a person to more deliberate ruminations, which are thought to have a direct relationship to growth.

Deliberate Ruminations

The second form of rumination that may be experienced posttrauma is deliberate rumination. This type of rumination is sometimes referred to as either constructive or reflective rumination. As the name suggests, deliberate rumination is purposeful, intentional thinking about a stressful or traumatic event. In the process of posttraumatic growth, deliberate ruminations are thought to be crucial and most productive when they are undertaken only *after* one is able to manage distress. If distress is not managed before deliberate ruminations, a person risks not being able to disengage from his or her pretrauma fundamental global beliefs and assumptions in the adaptive ways (Calhoun & Tedeschi, 1998, 2006). However, if distress is managed before a person's deliberate ruminating, then such ruminations are thought to lead to some psychologically beneficial experiences such as:

- Schema change
- Narrative development
- Posttraumatic growth (Calhoun & Tedeschi, 2006)

From the discussion on automatic and deliberate ruminations, one can already get a sense that not only the type of rumination is important to the process of posttraumatic growth, but the timing of automatic and deliberate ruminations is an important factor as well.

Timing of Ruminations

Ruminations are not necessarily time-limited. Ruminations of both forms may take place directly after a traumatic event, or they may continue long after the event has passed. With two forms of rumination (automatic and deliberate) already outlined, there become four different ways in which a person may experience ruminations:

1. Automatic ruminations soon after the event
2. Automatic ruminations still currently experienced sometime after the event
3. Deliberate ruminations soon after the event
4. Deliberate ruminations still currently experienced sometime after the event

In an empirical investigation of the theoretical sequence of ruminations that is thought to lead to growth (namely, automatic ruminations lead to deliberate ruminations and deliberate ruminations lead to posttraumatic growth), Taku, Cann, Tedeschi, and Calhoun (2009) explored the four different rumination categories in two different samples: a sample of 224 participants from the United States and a sample of 431 participants from Japan. The results from both studies indicated that while all types and timing combinations of ruminations had some degree of association with growth after trauma, the strongest predictor of growth in both samples was deliberate rumination still currently experienced sometime after the traumatic event. The researchers suggest that when working with clients sometime after a stressful or traumatic event, deliberate ruminations demand a therapist's attention:

> Identifying and supporting client's ruminations that may be constructive and deliberate, could significantly enhance the process of successful coping with highly challenging events and experiencing the positive byproducts of posttraumatic growth. (Taku et al., 2009, p. 135)

Likewise, in a recent study by Nightingale, Sher, and Hansen (2010) of 112 participants with HIV, the researchers explored the relationships of intrusive and deliberate ruminations at two points in time: (1) at the time of diagnosis and (2) at the time of the research study sometime after the traumatic event. The researchers' intention was to tease out the differences between type and timing of ruminations that tended to be related to growth and the type and timing of ruminations that tended to be related to psychological distress. Results indicated that:

- Intrusive cognitive processing at the time of diagnosis was directly related to posttraumatic growth, whereas current intrusive cognitive processing was related to psychological distress.
- Deliberate cognitive processing at the time of diagnosis was directly related to psychological distress, whereas current deliberate cognitive processing was directly related to post-traumatic growth.

The authors of the study suggest that automatic ruminations may feel both disruptive and unwanted; however, automatic rumination (which can include both positive and negative thoughts) experienced directly after trauma may be necessary for growth (Nightingale et al., 2010). Likewise, deliberate ruminations that may include a search for meaning directly after trauma may be less likely to lead to meaning and so be more likely to result in psychological distress rather than growth (Nightingale et al., 2010).

Stockton, Hunt, and Joseph (2011) also conducted two studies to investigate the type and time of ruminations that people have relative to growth. In the first study, the researchers examined the difference between brooding and reflective ruminations. Brooding ruminations most closely resemble automatic ruminations and were defined as "a passive focus on the causes and consequences of negative emotions or experiences, a repetitive comparison of one's current situation with some unachieved standard, and dwelling on obstacles that prevent one from overcoming problems" (p. 85). Reflective pondering more closely resembles deliberate ruminations and were defined as "a process by which the individual purposely turns inwards to engage in adaptive problem solving and is a relatively benign form of rumination distress" (p. 85).

In a sample of 212 adults, the results indicated that brooding ruminations had a negative association with growth. On the other hand, reflective pondering demonstrated a positive association with growth in instances when brooding ruminations were not present. In the second sample of 188 college students, results were somewhat similar in that a deliberate search for meaning and purposeful intention in processing a stressful or traumatic event and its consequences were related to experiences of posttraumatic growth. Further analysis revealed that trying to find meaning was more strongly related to posttraumatic growth than was a purposeful intention in processing the stressful or traumatic event. Although more deliberate forms of ruminations appear to be more closely related to posttraumatic growth, the authors suggest that utility of intrusive ruminations should not be dismissed, identifying "that certain types of intrusive thoughts that enable the individual to purposefully reflect on their experience might serve as a potential precursor to posttraumatic growth" (Stockton et al., 2011, p. 89).

All of the studies taken together support the understanding that although deliberate forms of ruminations appear to be essential for growth, intrusive ruminations have their place as well. In order to understand the utility of automatic and deliberate ruminations, along with the type of rumination, clinicians must also consider the timing of ruminations:

From the clinician's perspective, it is important to remember that, although much of the individuals' intrusive rumination is painfully undesirable and unwelcome, chewing on what has happened may well serve a highly useful adaptive function and may well be a necessary beginning to the process of posttraumatic growth. . . . [I]t may be that individuals who engage in high amounts of ruminative thought early on, but whose level of intrusive rumination is lower as weeks and months pass, are more likely to experience posttraumatic growth than persons whose level of aversive and intrusive rumination remains essentially unabated over extended periods of time. (Calhoun & Tedeschi, 1999, p. 19).

Positive Versus Negative Ruminations

A third characteristic of ruminations that may be of importance to the process of posttraumatic growth is whether the content of the ruminations a person experiences are overwhelmingly negative or positive. Linley and Joseph (2004) point out that cognitive appraisals about the event may include negative states of fear, anger, guilt, or shame or more positive states such as hope, joy, humor, and gratitude. The content of ruminations may be an indicator of growth such that people who experience more negative ruminations may be less likely to experience growth, whereas people with more positive ruminations may be more likely to experience growth. Calhoun and Tedeschi (1999) write,

Depending on the extent to which cognitive processing is focused on remembering positive pre-trauma events, on how the individual is going to cope, and on how to make sense or finding meaning in what happened, then one might expect not only less psychiatric distress but also higher levels of growth. (p. 18)

Empirically, Phelps, Williams, Raichle, Turner, and Ehde (2008) explored the difference in negative and positive cognitive processing and posttraumatic growth in a sample of 98 adults who had a recent limb amputation. Participants were assessed for cognitive processing at 1 month after amputation and for depression, posttraumatic stress disorder, and posttraumatic growth at both 6 and 12 months after amputation. Negative cognitive processing was assessed by such items as blaming, questioning "why me," thinking about what life would have been like if the amputation did not occur, and views of the self as a victim rather than a survivor (Phelps et al., 2008). Positive cognitive processing was assessed with items such as positive alteration in core beliefs, positive revisions of goals and priorities, and seeking beneficial aspects (Phelps et al., 2008).

Results found that while increased negative cognitive processing was related to increased depressive and posttraumatic stress disorder symptoms at 6 months after amputation, increased positive cognitive processing was related to decreased depressive symptoms at 6 and 12 months after amputation and increased posttraumatic growth at 12 months after amputation. The study supports that cognitive processing is a key targeted clinical intervention in the treatment of stress and trauma related to limb amputation (Phelps et al., 2008) and outlines the important distinctions between negative and positive forms of cognitive processing relative to the process of posttraumatic growth.

Gangstad, Norman, and Barton (2009) also examined the relationship between positive and negative forms of cognitive processing and posttraumatic growth in a sample of 60 adult survivors of stroke. Results indicated that growth was related to four aspects of cognitive processing:

1. Positive cognitive restructuring
2. Downward comparisons (comparing oneself to someone who is worse off than him or her)
3. Resolutions
4. Denial

Posttraumatic growth was not found to be related to cognitive processing that included regrets. Results also supported an understanding that has been and will be stressed throught this text: *Cognitive processing and subsequent growth is a process that takes time.* Researchers found that the relationship between growth and two forms of cognitive processing (*downward comparisons* and *resolutions*) became more positive with the passage of time (Gangstad et al., 2009), though exactly how much time is necessary for growth to elevate is still uncertain from the research.

Cognitive Processing and the Search for Meaning

Chapter 3 highlighted the great importance that meaning and meaning-making have in the process of moving through stress and trauma toward a sense of greater healing, peace, and perhaps growth. So then, ruminations that are specifically related in content to meaning-making or "sense-making" (Martin & Tesser, 1996) are important to turn a clinical ear toward when sitting with clients. Calhoun and Tedeschi's (2006) conceptualization of the importance of two different types of meaning in the content of client's posttrauma ruminations draws on the work of Janoff-Bulman and Frantz (1997), who indentified an important distinction between two different forms of sense-making. Both distinct forms of meaning may be part of cognitive processing related to growth.

The first form of sense-making that a client may engage in after trauma involves the search for meaning relative to the comprehensibility of the event. The case study example provided earlier in this chapter is an example of this form of meaning. The ruminations by the mother of the teenage girl who died from complications related to AIDS express that she was searching for meaning related to comprehending the event. She was attempting to fully understand that the event, the death of her daughter, did indeed take place. This form of meaning, meaning as comprehensibility, has often been associated with theories of posttraumatic stress disorder (Joseph & Linley, 2006). Meaning as comprehensibility of an event is very useful and necessary in order for clients to both manage the often great emotional distress that accompanies trauma, as well as in assisting clients to recognize that they are in fact truly able to cope with the traumatic event (Calhoun & Tedeschi, 2006). So while meaning as comprehensibility is certainly an important factor in clinical work, it is not thought to have a direct link to growth; instead, meaning as comprehensibility of a traumatic event is thought to be an *intermediate* step toward growth (Tedeschi & Calhoun, 2004).

The second form of sense-making that a client's ruminations may include is meaning as significance, sometimes understood as "meaningfulness." In contrast to meaning as comprehensibility, meaningfulness is a significantly more deliberate form of meaning-making that is thought to necessitate the experience of posttraumatic growth (Joseph & Linley, 2006). Meaningfulness involves not merely gaining a deep and real understanding that the traumatic event did indeed take place, but rather is related to the search for an understanding of the significance of the implications of the traumatic event in a person's life. We see meaningfulness in a client's deliberate ruminations around such questions as: What does my life mean now that this event has taken place? What does the event mean in regards to how I am to now view the world? and What does the event mean in regard to how I now view my life philosophy or spirituality that guides me day to day?

Coping is not a linear process, and cognitive processing of both forms of meaning may be interrelated and intertwined (Calhoun & Tedeschi, 1998). However, if distress from lack of comprehensibility of a trauma is too high, then more deliberate ruminations related to the significance of enduring the trauma and potential for growth as a result are probably not possible (Calhoun & Tedeschi, 2006). Additionally, as one starts to believe and accept that the trauma is a reality and part of the individual's life story, then meaningfulness is more possible to acquire, and so growth becomes more possible. Although meaning as comprehensibility and meaning as significance are distinct forms of meaning-making, the two forms do have a clinically important relationship worthy of a clinician's attention.

Ruminations and Clinical Work

The research on cognitive processing highlights a great deal of information that has clinical implications, but more research is essential to more fully flush out the intricacies of the relationship between the type, timing, and content of ruminations as it relates to clinical work. A good deal of research is still needed before clinicians have a greater understanding as to how and when to intervene with client ruminations in order to facilitate growth.

What appears to be key in working effectively with processing cognitions after stress and trauma is that the significant emotional distress that is often experienced and accompanies ruminations must be able to be managed by the client (Tedeschi & Calhoun, 2004). Without the ability to manage emotional distress, constructive cognitive processing becomes quite difficult. It is important then that clinicians attend to helping clients manage emotional distress, with the aim of not only decreasing negative stress and trauma-related symptomology but also increasing the likelihood for positive outcomes following growth. The management of emotional distress is possible through several interventions. As highlighted earlier in the chapter, expression of automatic and intrusive ruminations can lead to decreased emotional distress. Management of emotional distress is also possible through various body and mind focused relaxation techniques. Examples include guided meditations, visualization, various forms of exercise, and increased interpersonal communication.

Tedeschi and Calhoun (2006) suggest that perhaps the most useful role for clinicians to take at this point in time when working with clients who have experienced great stress and trauma is one of "expert companion." In part, being an expert companion is demonstrating the ability to encourage reflective cognitive processing of a client's stressful event to help a client to consider the ways in which he or she is reacting to the traumatic experience while maintaining the ability to not run away from moments in sessions in which a counselor is asked to contain a client's painful distress. In their words,

> So the expert companion is open to disclosure and encourages a reflective, analytical, conscious, emotionally-informed style of cognitive processing of trauma and avoids platitudes or other attempts to reassure that suppress this kind of trauma exposure. The expert companion must be able to tolerate distress in the survivor, although this kind of processing does not necessarily bring rapid relief. (Tedeschi & Calhoun, 2006, p. 297)

It is important to note as well, that to be an expert companion, clinicians must be attuned to the various ways in which a person's environment either encourages or discourages cognitive processing of events and the potential for growth. Culture can influence ruminations on two different levels. The first level of influence, the "proximate" level (Tedeschi & Calhoun, 2004), references the aspects of a person's environment, such as family, friends, and professional helpers. The second level of influence, the "distal" level (Tedeschi & Calhoun, 2004), references the culture at large. (Both of these levels are discussed in greater detail in Chapter 7.) Clinicians who work without an understanding of the ways in which societal themes or models for schemas of posttraumatic growth may exist—or not exist—as a person works to cognitively process a stressful or traumatic event are less equipped to take the role of expert companion.

Conclusion

Clients who have experienced trauma may enter therapy with at least one unrealistic and one realistic goal relative to ruminations: to return to a world pretrauma (which is impossible) and to decrease distress (which is completely possible). However, as research on posttraumatic growth has highlighted, distress is thought to initiate cognitive processing, so a certain amount of distress is needed in order for a person to engage with the meaning-making process and for growth to occur. Calhoun and Tedeschi (1999) warn that the process of posttraumatic growth can take a good deal of time. Operating without an awareness of this process can be counterproductive to growth. In the early stages, the clinician's role is to help clients to manage distress. However, clinicians need to be aware as they work with clients that some interventions can block the chances of growth (Calhoun & Tedeschi, 1999). They note:

> There is a fine line between helping the client manage distress and assisting the client to contemplate and mull over, which the traumatic events sets into motion. (p. 55)

So it would seem that it may be helpful for clinicians who are working with clients after stress and trauma to keep in mind the wisdom expressed in the words of an African proverb, "Smooth seas do not make skillful sailors." Clinicians do not want to make the sea any more difficult to manage, and in fact do want to assist clients in experiencing a calming of the sea, but in doing so clinicians do not want to ignore or diminish the possibility that clients may begin to understand that the crisis they have experienced and endured may be leading them to become more skillful sailors—a way of being that may be of value in numerous ways as they navigate the rest of their lives.

A Quote to Remember

From the clinician's perspective, it is important to remember that, although much of the individuals' intrusive rumination is painfully undesirable and unwelcome, chewing on what has happened may well serve a highly useful adaptive function and may well be a necessary beginning to the process of posttraumatic growth. . . . [I]t may be that individuals who engage in high amounts of ruminative thought early on, but whose level of intrusive rumination is lower as weeks and months pass, are more likely to experience posttraumatic growth than persons whose level of aversive and intrusive rumination remains essentially unabated over extended periods of time. (Calhoun & Tedeschi, 1999, p. 19)

Clinical Cornerstones of the Chapter

- Managing of emotional distress is an important component to effective cognitive processing that happens early on in the theraputic process. Management of distress is possible through helping clients to express either in writing or verbally their automatic or intrusive ruminations.
- Automatic ruminations may feel both disruptive and unwanted, but automatic rumination (which can include both positive and negative thoughts) experienced directly after trauma may be necessary for growth (Nightingale et al., 2010).
- Research has pointed to the great importance that identifying and supporting a client's deliberate ruminations experienced later in the coping process has in the facilitation of posttraumatic growth (Taku et al., 2009).
- When a client experiences deliberate ruminations that may include a search for meaning directly after trauma, meaning may not be found. The lack of an ability to find desired

meaning may then result in a client's experience of psychological distress (Nightingale et al., 2010).

• Tedeschi and Calhoun (2006) suggest that perhaps the most useful role for clinicians to take when working with clients who have experienced great stress and trauma is one of expert companion, encouraging reflective cognitive processing of the stressful event, in which a clinician helps a client to consider the ways in which the client is reacting to the traumatic experience.

Selected References

Phelps, L. F., Williams, R. H., Raichle, K. A., Turner, A. P., & Ehde, D. M. (2008). The importance of cognitive processing to adjustment in the first year following amputation. *Rehabilitation Psychology, 53,* 28–38.

This article explores the relationships between negative cognitive processing, positive cognitive processing, posttraumatic stress disorder, and posttraumatic growth. Results provide statistical evidence for the relationship between positive cognitive processing and growth, supporting Tedeschi and Calhoun's (2004) theory that deliberate cognitive processing is an important component of the outcome of posttraumatic growth.

Taku, K., Cann, A., Tedeschi, R. G., & Calhoun, L. G. (2009). Intrusive versus deliberate rumination in posttraumatic growth across US and Japanese samples. *Anxiety, Stress & Coping, 22,* 129–136.

This article examines the type and timing of ruminations and the relationship with posttraumatic growth in two different samples: one from the United States and one from Japan.

Tedeschi, R. L., & Calhoun, L. G. (2004). Posttraumatic growth: Conceptual foundations and empirical evidence. *Psychological Inquiry, 15,* 1–18.

This article from the researchers who developed the model of posttraumatic growth explains in detail the role that cognitive processing plays in development of posttraumatic growth. Additionally, it includes information on variables related to cognitive processing, such as distress and disclosure.

CHAPTER 5

POSITIVE EMOTIONS
AND GROWTH

Positive emotions are often not explicitly mentioned in models of posttraumatic growth. However, many researchers, including Calhoun and Tedeschi (2006), agree that though more research is definitely needed to better understand the ways in which positive emotions relate to posttraumatic growth, the research that exists is fairly certain that *positive emotions do share an important relationship with growth*. Research is now primarily examining positive emotions, with special attention to dispositional positive affect as a pretrauma personal characteristic of an individual that may be related to posttraumatic growth. It is important to note that dispositional positive affectivity is more of a trait rather than a temporary state characteristic (Calhoun & Tedeschi, 2006). Said differently, the form of positive affect that is being considered for its relationship to posttraumatic growth is less about a person's experience of joy in one moment of time and more about the overall tendency a person has to experience positive emotions such as joy throughout life.

Given this, several questions surround the relationship between positive emotions and growth that are worthy of examining:

- Does a person's pretrauma disposition to feel cheerful, to be open, and to be satisfied with life relate to whether a person experiences growth after traumatic experiences?

- Should we expect a client who presents with increased dispositional positive affect to be more likely to experience growth? And if so, why?
- Should a therapist assume that growth is illusion in clients who do not have characteristics or traits consistent with positive affect?
- Is there a causal link between growth and well-being such that positive emotions cause growth? Or, does growth cause positive emotions?

Research is moving toward answering such questions. The majority of the studies that do exist in the literature that examine positive emotions and growth (and really the majority of all growth studies in general) are correlational and cross-sectional. This means that the studies examine the relatedness of variables at one point in time. With such methodology we have a chicken and egg situation. We cannot determine if positive affect causes growth, if growth causes positive affect, or if both cases to some extent are true. There is certainly more research to be done in order to clarify the relationship between positive affect and growth. What is known at this point though is that: *Positive emotions speak to experiences of growth and have been associated with moving successfully through stress and crisis.* So then exploration of the relationship between positive emotions and growth is of use to the clinician, even at this early stage of research.

Definition of Positive Affectivity

Positive affectivity is defined by Peterson (2006) as the dispositional tendency to habitually experience positive emotions such as joy, interest, and alertness. Measures of positive affect attempt to capture the frequency with which a person feels such positive emotional states as cheerfulness, calmness and peacefulness, extreme happiness, and being satisfied and full of life (Brim & Featherman, 1998). Positive affect is also connected to the definition of subjective well-being—what one may consider the traditional definition of well-being that captures a specific aspect of a person's overall belief that life is good (Peterson, 2006). Specifically, subjective well-being is constructed as the combination of high levels of positive affect along with low negative affect and high life satisfaction (Diener, 1984).

We know that positive affect is associated with many positive aspects of life, such as increased social activity, friends, involvement in organizations, being happily married, finding enjoyment in vocation, religiosity and spirituality, life satisfaction (Peterson, 2006), and happiness (Fredrickson & Joiner, 2002). Positive affect has also been found to be associated with several positive physical health indicator,s such as improved immune system functioning (Davidson et al., 2003), improved cardiovascular activity (Fredrickson, Mancuso, Branigan, & Tugade, 2000), and longevity (Danner, Snowdon, & Friesen, 2001). We see from the aforementioned correlations that positive emotions are related to healthy, meaningful, growth-oriented experiences in life. A deeper look into positive emotions makes it abundantly clear that positive emotions possess a good deal of power in an individual's emotional life.

The Power of Positive Emotions

For some time, psychology was solitary symptom-focused and as such exclusively examined negative emotions. However, in the 1990s, in the wake of the positive psychology movement, Barbara Fredrickson and colleagues began giving specific and focused attention to the power of positive emotions. Until the positive psychology movement, positive emotions did not receive any truly focused attention. Rather, negative emotions captured the attention in ways that positive emotions did not. However, many people's research efforts, including Fredrickson's, have permanently changed the field. Fredrickson documented in her groundbreaking experiments evidence to support her innovative theory of positive emotions, known as the *Broaden and Build Theory of Positive Emotions* (1998, 2001). Her theory suggests that positive emotions are not merely a lack of negative emotions. Rather, they are distinct from negative emotions and uniquely powerful in their own right. In fact, positive emotions operate in a completely different way from negative emotions. Her theory outlines how negative emotions are evolutionary-based to elicit a survival action. When we feel fear, we desire to flee. When we feel anger, we desire to attack. Negative emotions purposefully constrict our thoughts and actions to the survival technique response linked to the emotion. For example, if we were to meet a lion in the wild, it is not the time for creative exploration. It is the time to run!

Positive emotions, however, do not operate in the same way. Instead of limiting our scope of attention and the actions to which negative emotions are linked, positive emotions widen one's thoughts and actions so as to broaden our scope of attention and behavioral repertoires (Fredrickson, 2001). Positive emotions set our thoughts and actions free to creatively explore the possibilities that life holds. Positive emotions urge and encourage us to do such things as play, explore, take in new information, savor, share, and expand the self (Fredrickson, 2001).

Fredrickson (2001) uses the metaphor of positive emotions as "vehicles for individual growth" that encourage personal development. This form of *broadening* compounds over time and *builds* physical, intellectual, social, and psychological resources. In doing so, positive emotions are not merely markers of psychological flourishing, though they are this as well. Positive emotions are also capable of *producing* psychological flourishing (Fredrickson, 2001).

In one of Fredrickson's many studies, Fredrickson, Cohn, Coffey, Pek, and Finkel (2008) examined the effects of positive emotions induced through loving-kindness meditation and their abilities to build an individual's personal resources. In a randomized study of 139 adults, half of the participants practiced six 60-minute group meditation exercises over a period of 7 weeks while the other half did not. The meditation focused on directing love and compassion toward the self and others.

Results in the study were important for our purpose here because they found that participants in the meditation group experienced increases in daily experiences of positive emotions, which led to increases in positive personal resources such as mindfulness, purpose in life, and social support. Increases in personal resources were in turn predictive of increased satisfaction with life and decreased depressive symptoms. Additionally, increased positive personal resources led to decreases in indicators of illness. Together, the results provide evidence for the beneficial relationships among positive emotions, positive psychological resources, and indicators of well-being.

Along with these relationships, also of crucial importance to understanding the power of positive emotions relative to posttraumatic growth is the idea that the benefits of positive emotions are *not momentary*. Rather, the benefits have long-lasting implications for well-being that are experienced long after the positive emotion has been experienced. Positive emotions serve as a lasting personal resource that can be called on at a later time, in different emotional states, as needed (Fredrickson, 2000). And, as is obviously important to us here, such states may be times of stress, crisis, and trauma.

Fredrickson's research also speaks of two other ideas that are important to positive emotions and how one may experience stress and crisis. The first is the "undoing hypothesis," which, as the name implies, suggests that positive emotions may not only build positive personal resources, but they may also have the ability to undo the effects of negative emotions. Second, Fredrickson's research also speaks of how positive emotions can trigger an upward spiral, a self-perpetuating cycle (Garland et al., 2010), where the experience of positive emotions can predict subsequent positive emotional experiences.

Fredrickson et al. (2003) conducted a small study of 46 U.S. college students who had experienced the stress and trauma of the September 2001 terrorist attacks. Evaluating the students before and after the September 2001 terrorist attacks, researchers found that in resilient people, positive emotions can buffer depressive symptoms. Additionally, and most important in times of crisis, the connection between precrisis resiliency characteristics and posttrauma growth is accounted for by the fact that resilient people tend to experience an increased frequency of positive emotions. Rather than crisis being an experience that draws down a person's psychological resources, more frequent experiences of positive emotions after a crisis is related to increases in psychological resources for growth (Fredrickson et al., 2003).

Thus, the research on positive emotions provides a frame for imagining the ways in which dispositional tendency toward positive emotions may encourage positive emotional responses to stress and trauma in a way that people who do not possess the same degree of positive emotions may not respond. There appear to be obvious relationships between positive emotions in general and positive affect specifically and the ability to experience growth after trauma. Therefore, with the broader perspective that positive emotions encourage, perhaps internal growth may be more apt to occur.

To compliment Fredrickson's research, King, Hicks, Krull, and Del Gaiso (2006) also provide related evidence in a series of six studies that suggest positive emotions may predispose an individual to find and feel more meaning in life. Because meaning-making is one of the frames for understanding where growth experiences come from (Park, 2004), this is important.

Additionally, the ideas of exploration, taking in new information, and expansion of the self are all in line with the key concepts of posttraumatic growth. Trauma shatters assumptions and demands a period of exploration of what beliefs the client holds about the self, others, and the world. Posttraumatic growth represents new understandings based on new information. Expansion of self in positive ways is growth. With these parallels, one wonders then if growth is possible without positive emotions. Indeed, they may very well be necessary.

In line with research suggesting that positive emotions can have an important role to play in times of stress and trauma, it is important for both researchers and clinicians to maintain a balanced approach in their work by understanding that both positive and negative emotions have important roles in the process of stress and coping (Folkman, 2008). Both positive and negative emotions deserve attention in the clinical hour. It has been suggested that:

> For both researchers and clinicians, it is important to maintain a balanced perspective regarding the role of positive emotions in the stress process. This stress process is strongly characterized by negative emotions, and the inclusion of positive emotions in the model is just that, inclusion. However, the evidence suggests that the positive emotions have important adaptational significance and that these emotions are generated by identifiable coping processes. Stress researchers need to include positive emotions in their studies to learn more about how people generate and sustain them and to further explore their adaptational significance in relation to physiological, psychological, and social outcomes. Clinicians need to give attention to positive emotions with their clients, and explore the sources of such emotions and how to generate and sustain them. This attention to positive emotions will address the imbalance between stress research and clinical practice that has resulted from decades of nearly exclusive concern with the negative emotions. (Folkman, 2008, p. 12)

Empirical Connections Among Positive
Affectivity, Well-Being, and Growth

The French painter Henri Matisse declared, "There are always flow-ers for those who want to see them." However, while Matisse's quo-tation suggests perhaps an equal ability of all individuals to experi-ence beauty in the world around us dependent only on one's desire, research suggests that positive emotions may play a role in a person's capacity to see the flowers that begin to bloom in times of crisis.

A review of posttraumatic growth literature indicates that post-traumatic growth has been consistently associated with positive affect (Helgeson et al., 2006; Linley & Joseph, 2004) and positive well-being (Helgeson et al., 2006). The largest investigation of the relationship between positive well-being (a definition that includes positive affect) and posttraumatic growth was completed by Hel-geson et al. (2006) as part of a meta-analysis of 87 studies from 77 articles. Helgeson defined the construct of well-being as the combination of positive affect, self-esteem, and life satisfaction. The researchers' criterion for inclusion of research studies was such that they used only published, peer-reviewed studies and analyzed only cross-sectional relationships. They included research that took place in Western cultures, was published before 2005, and was available in an electronic database where posttraumatic growth was clearly defined and measured. They used only articles written in English, those that included a measure of either physical or mental health, or where participants over 18 years of age had clearly experienced a stressful or traumatic event. The research was quite significant, including a total of 2,268 participants across the studies in which positive well-being was examined.

Results from the meta-analysis suggest several important points. First, there was an overall significant relationship between positive well-being and growth such that people who reported increased levels of well-being also reported increased levels of growth. Second, well-being had a stronger association with growth when compared to such factors as depression and intrusive-avoidant thoughts. Third, positive affect specifically was clearly related to posttraumatic growth (Helgeson et al., 2006). Interestingly, the researchers also discovered an important caveat to the relationship between positive affect and growth. When more than 2 years were allowed to pass after a person experienced a traumatic event, posttraumatic growth was *more strongly* related to greater positive affect as well as lower depression. The importance of the passage of time in the relationship between growth and positive affect has clear clinical implications that will be discussed shortly.

In addition to the cross-sectional (or one point in time) analysis considered in the meta-analysis, several specifically longitudinal-designed studies have also assessed the relationship between positive affect and growth. For instance, Abraido-Lanza, Guier, and Colon (1998) examined the connections between positive affect and the ability to find something beneficial or gained as a result of experiencing physical illness in a 3-year longitudinal design that consisted of a sample of 66 Latina women with arthritis. Researchers found that positive affect at baseline had a direct effect on growth, suggesting that people who experience more positive emotions are more likely to find benefits from their illness 3 years later. Similarly, Carver and Antoni (2004) examined the longitudinal effects of growth and positive affect in a sample of 96 women who were first assessed at their initial stage of breast cancer and then assessed 4 to 7 years later. Initial benefit finding predicted increased positive affect at the follow-up assessment.

Boyraz and Efstathiou (2011) examined a slightly more advanced aspect of the relationship between positive affect and growth, exploring whether positive affect mediated (accounted for) the found relationships between ruminations, self-reflections, and growth. In a sample of 187 bereaved women, the researchers found that positive affect partially mediated or was partially responsible for the relationships such that those who engaged in self-reflection reported higher levels of positive affect, which in turn was related to experiences of growth. Additionally, those who engaged in rumination reported lower levels of positive affect, which in turn was related to fewer experiences of growth. The results support the idea that positive affect is in part responsible for why people experience growth after stress and trauma.

Overall, there are two potential explanations for the significant relationships found between posttraumatic growth and positive affect supported by the empirical literature. Positive affect may:

- Support successful cognitive processing of a traumatic event
- Reflect traits such as dispositional hope or optimism (Lechner et al., 2008, p. 215)

As was discussed in Chapter 4 and is discussed in Chapter 6, theory suggests and research supports that effective cognitive process and pretrauma personality characteristics are key aspects of the development of posttraumatic growth. Still, further research is necessary to more deeply understand the relationship of positive affect and growth after trauma.

Conflicting Data to Consider

Although these studies suggest a relationship between posttraumatic growth and positive affect, a few studies provide seemingly contradictory results. For example, a 3-month longitudinal study of 55 posttreatment colorectal survivors conducted by Salsman et al. (2009) found no relationship between positive affect and posttraumatic growth, either at the initial assessment at the start of the study or at the 3-month follow-up assessment. One possible explanation for the lack of relationship could be that perhaps 3 months, while an adequate amount of time in the aforementioned longitudinal studies, may not be sufficient enough time for positive affect to correlate with posttraumatic growth in other samples. To find relationships between growth and positive affect may require a period of not months, but perhaps as much as several years (Salsman et al., 2009; Schaefer & Moos, 1998). Therefore, studies that happen at least 1 year after a traumatic event may support evidence of a relationship between posttraumatic growth and positive affect, whereas studies that correlate posttraumatic growth and positive affect less than 1 year after the stressful life event may find no significant relationship. This timing has obvious potential clinical implications to be discussed.

Clinical Implications

As has been alluded to earlier, there are several essential clinical implications of the research on positive emotions. Generally, clinicians need to be aware of the role that positive emotions play in coping with stress and trauma. The role is very different than the role of negative emotions. To be aware of the role is not to take a Pollyanna view, but to be open and aware that positive emotions encourage engagement with the world in a more open and creative way. They have a purpose that is not the opposite of negative emotions, but rather, uniquely their own.

Second, if the connection between posttraumatic growth and positive affect enhances over time, then it may be necessary for adequate time to pass following the trauma before assessing the relationships. Clinicians need to be aware that in the treatment of trauma victims, they must take care *not* to look for or expect a connection between positive affect and growth too soon, or as has been stated before, to even look for growth at all, even in clients who report high levels of dispositional positive affect prestress and pretrauma. The Dalai Lama is quoted as saying, "From the very core of our being we desire contentment." We are people made to experience positive emotions. It is who we are. However, sometimes, negative things happen that can challenge our expression of positive emotion. *Our desire for contentment and that of our clients' contentment must keep us vigilant from pushing or trying to see connections of growth and positive affect that is not there, or not there yet.* (This point cannot be emphasized enough.)

As we now understand from the research on time, positive affect, and trauma, it can take years to begin to see the relationships between trauma and positive affect. This suggests that patience on the part of both the client and the clinician is critical for growth to be seen. There is a real danger in inordinately pushing for connections between growth and positive affect in the early stages of trauma and stress work or in seeking to force the client into a seemingly ideal therapeutic position before the timing becomes possible. Though this therapeutic error may seem self-evident, unfortunately it is not, especially in the case of clinicians who are aware of the promise of the literature on posttraumatic growth, but who may not possess a full appreciation of the pacing and timing involved in achieving this promise with clients.

Staying present in the moment is a central concept to achieving this fine balance. Several techniques may help therapists to remain mindful with clients and not get ahead of where they are or move to a place that would not be valuable for the client. Such techniques include a practice of centering that involves:

- Bringing awareness to your breath in the present moment
- Bringing awareness to your body in the present moment
- Quieting your fears that you are not a good enough therapist
- Disequating success with posttraumatic growth (for some clients success is a return to baseline experiences)
- Remembering it is not your job to take away a client's pain, but to be personally and professionally *faithful* as a clinician
- Remembering that it is not your job to make your client grow

• Quieting your desires for the quick removal of client pain without silencing your hope
• Listening to your client with new ears (not ears that hold history or expectation)
• Discouraging any forms of judgment about where the client is at present
• Encouraging acceptance of where the client is in the moment

Incorporating time before sessions to reflect on these practices and being certain to leave enough time before and after sessions can help us in the therapeutic role to encourage a mindfulness and availability to the client, which is a primary goal in the treatment of any client—and *especially* those who have encountered severe trauma.

However, knowing that positive emotions are so powerful, we must not overlook the obvious clinical question then of "How do we foster positive emotions so that we engage in an upward spiral of positive emotions and not the downward spiral of negative emotions?" There are a few steps we can take. First, we must understand that we each possess the capacity to experience both positive and negative emotions. Both types of emotions serve a function. We cannot eradicate negative emotions to the exclusion of positive emotions. In fact, research from Fredrickson and Losada (2005) has found that too much positive emotion in ratio to negative emotion is not necessarily good for well-being. Of course, too little positive emotion is not good either. In fact, the researchers calculated a mathematical ratio that supported the necessity for a person to experience at least 2.9 positive emotions and no more than 11.6 positive emotions for every one negative emotion in order to experience psychological flourishing. Knowing the ratio range can be helpful in clinical situations as we listen to the positive and negative emotions that are shared by our clients in session. What the ratio does not speak to, however, is how one fosters positive emotions clinically.

One resource in this area that may be useful for clinicians' further exploration is a work by Sonja Lyubomirsky (2007), *The How of Happiness*. In her book she shares a belief backed by research that positive emotions can make a person happier. She cites expressing gratitude and visioning your best possible self as pathways to increasing positive emotion (Sheldon & Lyubomirsky, 2006).

In a similar vein, Fredrickson (2000) suggests ways that clients can foster positive emotions. She specifically mentions the beneficial role of:

- Relaxation training such as:
  - Yoga
  - Meditation
  - Guided imagery exercise
- Finding positive meaning through:
  - Reframing adverse events in a positive light (also called positive reappraisal)
  - Infusing ordinary events with positive value
  - Pursuing and attaining realistic goals
- Invoking empathy, amusement, or interest

Daisaku Ikeda, a Japanese peace activist, is quoted as saying, "With love and patience, nothing is impossible." Such words, along with the aforementioned suggestions, are reminders that the therapist's stance matters immensely in the clinical setting. Sitting patiently with clients, not rushing them to be in a space or experience an emotion, or to explore a clinical theme, honors the process that is necessary for healing after stress and trauma. Doing so may also help clients to hold the possibility of experiencing positive well-being and growth after stress and trauma.

It is clear from the literature on positive emotions, trauma, and growth that the empirical connections should not raise the expectations we place on our clients, but we still need and must not place any limit on the elevation of our hope for our clients' well-being and the well-being of our world. The possibility of significant post-traumatic growth often relies on this attitude on the part of the clinician.

A Quote to Remember

For both researchers and clinicians, it is important to maintain a balanced perspective regarding the role of positive emotions in the stress process. This stress process is strongly characterized by negative emotions, and the inclusion of positive emotions in the model is just that, inclusion. However, the evidence suggests that the positive emotions have important adaptational significance and that these emotions are generated by identifiable coping processes. Stress researchers need to include positive emotions in their studies to learn more about how people generate and sustain them and to further explore their adaptational significance in relation to physiological, psychological, and social outcomes. Clinicians need to give attention to positive emotions with their clients, and explore the sources of such emotions and how to generate and sustain them. This attention to positive emotions will address the imbalance between stress research and clinical practice that has resulted from decades of nearly exclusive concern with the negative emotion (Folkman, 2008, p. 12).

Clinical Cornerstones of the Chapter

- Honor the positive emotions that exist in the stress and coping process, along with the negative emotions. To accomplish this we must be sensitive to their appearance and react in ways that, while not patronizing, reinforce their presence (i.e., having the client discuss or give illustrations of positive emotions as well as the results of having experienced them).

- Remain open and patient to the process of posttraumatic growth, as it can take up to 2 years or more for clients to experience the growth that is connected to positive emotions. Patience is one of the key elements of the psychological treatment of persons who have been traumatized.
- Incorporate practices that encourage your ability to stay in the present moment. Reading on mindfulness so as to open up a broad array of ways for both the clinician and client to practice both informally and formally would be very helpful.
- Although we need to lower our expectations of growth, we need not lower our hope. When working with traumatized clients, a stance of hopeful openness on the part of the clinician is a key to enabling posttraumatic growth if it is possible to achieve this with the client.

Selected References

Folkman, S. (2008). The case for positive emotions in the stress process. *Anxiety, Stress, & Coping, 21,* 3–14.
  This paper summarizes the current relationships between positive emotions in the process of stress and coping.
Fredrickson, B. (2000). Cultivating positive emotions to optimize health and well-being. *Prevention and Treatment, 3.*
  Fredrickson, a leading researcher in the psychological study of positive emotion, presents information on how to foster the development of positive emotions clinically.
Fredrickson, B. (2001). The role of positive emotions in positive psychology: The broaden and build theory of positive emotions. *The American Psychologist, 56,* 218–226.
  Fredrickson's paper that explains her ground-breaking theory of positive emotions: The Broaden and Build Theory. The article provides both a theoretical argument as well as empirical evidence to support her theory.

Helgeson, V. S., Reynolds, K. A., & Tomich, P.L. (2006). A meta-analytic review of benefit finding and growth. *Journal of Consulting and Clinical Psychology, 74*, 797–816.

This article is a meta-analysis that includes 77 articles and 87 different studies, which together support the statistical relationships among trauma, positive affect, well-being, and growth.

Wicks, R. (2008). *The resilient clinician*. New York, NY: Oxford University Press.

This book contains a chapter on mindfulness, as well as a selected bibliography on the topic that is useful for further reading.

CHAPTER 6

PERSONALITY AND PERSONAL ATTRIBUTES

We know from the research on posttraumatic growth outlined in Chapter 4 that cognitive processing, or intentional engagement with the stressful or traumatic event, appears to be one of the factors that is a prerequisite for posttraumatic growth to occur (Calhoun & Tedeschi, 2006; Stanton, Bower, & Low, 2006). Without cognitive engagement with the stressor, nothing new can be experienced, although some people cognitively engage with a traumatic event in ways that lead to posttraumatic growth and others do not. Whether a person engages with processing the traumatic event in ways that lead to posttraumatic growth experiences may be partly a result of personality characteristics. The question becomes one of what types of personalities and personality attributes make engagement with stressors and posttraumatic growth process more plausible.

Research suggests that our personality shapes how we experience the world. Research on happy personalities indicates that personality can color people's perceptions of events and even work toward returning a person to a pre-event level of well-being after a major life event (DeNeve & Cooper, 1998). Personality and personality attributes are factors that should not be ignored both in research and in clinical practice related to stress, trauma, and growth.

Several models of personality can be used in the exploration of growth. Perhaps one of the more useful ways of examining how personality relates to posttraumatic growth is the Five-Factor Model of personality, which considers personality not from a pathological vantage point but from the viewpoint of health.

The Five-Factor Model of Personality

The concept of the Five-Factor Model of Personality can be dated back to a 1933 presidential address at the American Psychological Association meeting by Louis Thurstone (Digman, 1996). Dropped at the time by Thurstone in pursuit of different work, a somewhat complex history of the development of the model followed (see *The Five-Factor Model of Personality: Theoretical Perspectives* edited by Jerry S. Wiggins, 1996 for a more complete explanation of the history and development of the Five-Factor Model). Simply put, the model is a descriptive classification of personal traits comprised in five broad domains (McCrae & Costa, 1991). Unlike other personality indicators that are categorical in nature (e.g., the Myers-Briggs Indicator), the Five-Factor Model supposes that each person possesses to some degree or another each of the following five domains:

1. **Neuroticism:** The degree to which a person experiences negative affects and is prone to experience psychological distress
2. **Extraversion:** The degree to which one can tolerate being around other people and directs personal energy towards others
3. **Openness:** The degree to which one is open to, appreciates, and seeks life experiences
4. **Agreeableness:** The degree to which one has an orientation towards others as indicated by one's tendency for certain types of interpersonal interactions
5. **Conscientiousness:** The degree to which one is personally organized, motivated, and able to carry out tasks and work towards goals (Costa & McCrae, 1992)

On the Neuroticism, Extraversion, Openness personality indicator (NEO-PI-R), NEO Personality Interview Revised (Costa & McCrae, 1992), each of the personality domains consist of several facets. Neuroticism includes facets such as anxiety, hostility, depression, self-consciousness, impulsiveness, and vulnerability. A person who scores low in this domain may be described as calm, relaxed, or resilient (Costa & McCrae, 1992). A person who scores high in this domain may be described as apprehensive, worrying, and fearful. Extraversion includes the facets of warmth, gregariousness, assertiveness, activity, excitement-seeking, and positive emotions. Persons with low scores tend to be cold, cautious, and serious. Persons with high scores in this domain tend to be outgoing, energetic, and cheerful (Costa & McCrae, 1992). Openness includes the facets of fantasy, aesthetics, feelings, actions, ideas, and values. Persons with high scores on openness tend to be curious and willing to consider unconventional ideas. Persons who score low on openness tend to be conventional and conservative in their world outlook (Costa & McCrae, 1992). Agreeableness includes the facets of trust, straightforwardness, altruism, modesty, compliance, and tender-mindedness. Persons who score low on agreeableness tend to be self-minded, competitive, antagonistic, and leery of others' intentions. People who score high on agreeableness tend to be altruistic, cooperative, and sympathetic towards others, desire to be helpful, and hold a belief in others' desires to be helpful (Costa & McCrae, 1992). Finally, conscientiousness includes the facets of competence, order, dutifulness, achievement, self-discipline, and deliberation (Costa & McCrae, 1992). Persons who score low on conscientiousness tend to be more lackadaisical in their organization and movement toward a task. Persons who score high on conscientiousness tend to be determined, purposeful, reliable, and scrupulous (Costa & McCrae, 1992).

Personality, as understood by the conceptualization of the Five-Factor Model, is considered to have an enduring and pervasive influence in one's life that either does not change, or minimally changes, throughout one's adult life (Costa & McCrae, 1992; McCrae & Costa, 1991). Relative to the topic at hand, the Five-Factor Model of personality is thought to be related to a person's experience of well-being and, most importantly, to affect the way in which individuals react to stressful experiences (McCrae & Costa, 1986, 1991).

Personality Factors and Posttraumatic Growth

There is research to support associations with posttraumatic growth and the domains of personality outlined in the Five-Factor Model. All of the domains, save neuroticism, have been found to have positive associations with growth; neuroticism has been found to have a negative association (Lechner, Stoelb, & Antoni, 2008; Linley & Joseph, 2004). Tedeschi and Calhoun (2004) suggest, however, that the relationship between personality and growth is modest. Most significantly, those who are more extraverted and those who are more open to new experiences pretrauma may be more likely to experience growth after trauma (Calhoun & Tedeschi, 1999). Their argument suggests that the personality characteristics of extraversion and openness (and specifically the facet of openness to feelings [Calhoun & Tedeschi, 2006]) may allow a person to experience more positive affect during stressful and traumatic experiences, which may allow a person to engaged in cognitive processing more effectively (Tedeschi & Calhoun, 2004).When considering the total number of research studies that exist in the field on posttraumatic growth, and the total number of studies that include personality domains as factors in the investigation, the empirical research that includes personality variables and posttraumatic growth is somewhat limited. However, what follows are two examples of studies that speak to the relationship between personality domains and growth.

Australian researchers Wilson and Boden (2008) included personality in their examination of posttraumatic growth, along with the variables of religiosity and social support. The sample consisted of 104 predominantly female participants from two different populations: (a) undergraduate students in psychology and anthropology classes at the University of Southern Queensland and (b) residents of Toowoomba, Queensland, Australia. The study found that posttraumatic growth significantly correlated with extraversion, and to a lesser degree with conscientiousness, along with the number of social supports a participant had and the participant's religious orientation. A hierarchical regression analysis examined the amount of variance that the personality factors explained in posttraumatic growth after accounting for the variance explained by social support and religious orientation. The results indicated that extraversion alone accounted for 11% of the variance of posttraumatic growth that was not explained by social support or religious orientation. The results suggest that *a person who can tolerate being around other people to a greater degree will likely experience a greater degree of growth.* Likewise, the results support Tedeschi and Calhoun's (2004) analysis that extraversion is one of the more significant factors of personality relative to growth after stress and trauma.

In a study by Garnefski, Kraaij, Schroevers, and Somsen (2008) of 138 medical patients who had experienced a myocardial infarction between 3 to 12 months before the study, researchers examined the extent to which posttraumatic growth could be explained by personality factors. The study found that extraversion and conscientiousness had positive associations with growth, and neuroticism had a negative association. They also provide evidence to support the idea that personality had a modest relationship to growth. For when put into the context of other factors, personality's relationship to growth appeared to be weaker than the relationship of growth related to a person's level of cognitive processing, but stronger than the relationship between growth and a person's psychological health. Such relationships were found over and above the potential effects of such characteristics as gender, age, and the time that had passed since the stressful event (the myocardial infarction). The results bring up an interesting thought about the importance of personality in clinical work. Although it is common for clinicians to assess for the present state of psychological health in counseling, it is less common for clinicians to assess for personality in the clinical intake sessions. The results suggest that some amount of intervention with regard to personality may be warranted.

Tedeschi and Calhoun suggest (2006) that in order to access personality-related information about a client, a clinician could ask one of the following questions or statements for the client to consider:

- What were you like before this happened?
- What has been your typical way of responding to a problem?
- What was the hardest thing you have had to handle before all this happened? How did you address that?
- Have there been instances where you sought out new experiences?
- Think of a time when you did manage to get through difficulty. (p. 294)

Such questions allow a therapist to achieve a greater understanding of the tendencies a client has related to personality factors such as *openness to experiences* or *extraversion* without having to give an assessment. However, for therapists who wish to give a personality assessment, McCrae and Costa (1992) suggest that the NEO-PI-R is a useful assessment for counselors to give because of the ease with which it can be integrated into therapy. The NEO-PI-R, as mentioned earlier, measures normal personality rather than psychopathology. Questions are not included in regard to suicidal or homicidal ideation or hearing voices that may be offputting to some clients (though suicidal and homicidal ideation is important to assess for clinically in some way). Rather, the assessment questions focus on the degrees to which personality traits aforementioned (e.g., cheerfulness, warmth, hostility) resonate with the client's view of him or herself.

Personal Attributes/Factors

Beyond the Five-Factor Model, several personality attributes or factors have been examined in regard to their relationship with growth. Optimism is one such factor. It has been suggested that optimism may be the most frequently studied personality trait for its relationship to growth (Lechner et al., 2008), and at least modest relationships have been found in nearly all of the studies that include this variable (Stanton, Bower, & Low, 2006). *Dispositional optimism* is defined as "the global expectation that good things will be plentiful in the future and bad things scarce" (Peterson, 2006, p. 119). Not surprisingly, perhaps, research has linked people who tend to have higher levels of dispositional optimism with increased likeliness to report experiences of posttraumatic growth. Tedeschi and Calhoun (2004) suggest that optimism may be an important personality characteristic to have in order to engage in cognitive processing effectively. Citing the work of Aspinwall, Richter, and Hoffman (2001), Tedeschi and Calhoun suggest that optimism may allow a person to cognitively engage with material that is controllable and to disengage with material that is uncontrollable.

While optimism may be a useful personality characteristic in the process of growth, paradoxically, we also know that stress and trauma may threaten or challenge a person's optimism (Peterson, 2006). So then, while optimism may enhance perceptions of posttraumatic growth (Lechner et al., 2008), its livelihood is also threatened in the very experience for which it is useful.

Several studies on posttraumatic growth have included a look at optimism. In the meta-analysis by Helgeson et al. (2006), the authors examined the relationship between optimism and posttraumatic growth. A total of 11 studies and 2,628 participants across the studies suggested an association between greater optimism and benefit finding. Similarly, in a meta-analysis of 39 studies by Linley and Joseph (2004), the same relationship was found.

Antoni et al. (2001) examined the relationship and impact of optimism and growth in a sample of 100 women who had been newly diagnosed with Stage 0 to II breast cancer. A subsample of the participants was assigned to an intervention group, participating in a 10-week (2-hour per week) group session in which cognitive-behavioral stress management interventions were used. Results of the study indicated that for women who participated in the group intervention, there was a reported increase in growth and increase in optimism at the end of the 10-week session. The increased levels of growth and optimism were also still present at a 3-month follow-up. In the study, the greatest increases took place for women who started with low levels of optimism. Interestingly, changes in growth and optimism modestly tracked each other over time, with follow-up measures correlating significantly (Antoni et al., 2001).

Optimism has also been linked to posttraumatic growth in what could be categorized as some of the most extreme cases of trauma as well. For example, Feder et al. (2008) examined the relationship between the two constructs in a sample of 30 males who were former prisoners of war (POWs) during the Vietnam War. As POWs, the sample endured experiences such as torture and prolonged solitary confinement that lasted as long as 2 to 3 years for some prisoners. In the sample, results supported that increased optimism was predictive of increased posttraumatic growth. When a solider presented with high levels optimism, he also presented with high levels of growth.

There are two important notes to summarize in the study of optimism and growth. The first note is that the studies on the relationships between optimism and growth are cross-sectional, so directionality cannot be assumed. Although it has been hypothesized that pretrauma dispositional optimism increases the likelihood of posttraumatic growth, it may very well be that the ability to find benefits posttrauma increases one's levels of optimism. Continued research will help in answering such a question and inform meaningful clinical practice.

Second, it is important to note in the research as well that optimism is a related but separate construct from posttraumatic growth (Stanton et al., 2006; Tedeschi & Calhoun, 2004). This means that there is a relationship between optimism and growth, but it takes more than optimism to find benefits of enduring stress and trauma. Optimism is relevant in the process, but it alone does not account for the psychological process. This is an important point clinically, because a client who presents with pessimistic thinking should not be ruled out for the potential to experience growth.

Self-Esteem/Self-Efficacy

A person's concept of self is the total thoughts and feelings that one has toward the self (Rosenberg, 1986). Two aspects of a person's self-concept are self-esteem and self-efficacy. Self-esteem and self-efficacy are related but distinct constructs that speak to the thoughts and beliefs people have about their abilities to successfully function in any given life situation. *Self-esteem* is defined as an individual's attitude or orientation, either positive or negative, toward the self (Rosenberg, 1986). *Self-efficacy* has been defined as "the belief in one's capabilities to organize and execute the courses of action required to manage prospective situations" (Bandura, 1995, p. 2).

Research studies have given some attention to the potential connections between self-esteem, self-efficacy, and growth after stress and trauma. For example, Schulz and Mohamed (2004) examined the relationship between self-efficacy and growth in a sample of 105 German cancer patients. As well, Carpenter, Brockopp, and Andrykowski (1999) examined the relationship between self-esteem and positive transformation in a sample of 60 female cancer survivors and 60 females who served as a control group. Both studies support that high levels of self-efficacy and self-esteem are related to high levels of growth and transformation. This suggests that the thoughts people have in regard to their ability to successfully function and their deep-rooted sense of lovability and worthiness is relative to experiencing growth. People who construct a sense of self as capable and lovable are more likely to engage cognitively with a stress or trauma that leads to new, positive understandings of their self, others, and the world. However, while psychologically healthy people may have a slightly inflated sense of personal self-control in life, it has also been suggested that people who have *extremely* high beliefs in their self and their control over life may have a tendency to find extreme stress and trauma more difficult to cope with (Tedeschi & Calhoun, 1995), because stress and trauma may break apart one's previously held assumptions of what one can and cannot control in life.

Clinical Applications

Although there is certainly some debate in the field, in general, the five factors of personality are understood to be enduring aspects of personality that are not likely to change over time (McCrae & Costa, 1991). So then, if personality domains are by definition off the table (other than for assessing them to get a broader understanding of the client, as indicated previously in the chapter), we turn to examine the personality attributes that are understood to have the potential for more fluidity and possibly increase or decrease based on interventions. We turn to optimism first.

Renowned positive psychology researcher, Martin Seligman (2006), in his book, *Learned Optimism: How to Change Your Mind and Your Life*, explained that optimism is a personality attribute that can be increased or decreased based on several factors within a person's control. He shares that pessimistic beliefs can be met with both disputation and distraction. Seligman notes that disputation is more effective when considering the long-term implications of the techniques (2006). People can learn to argue with themselves, searching for evidence of alternatives and their implications on the usefulness of beliefs that are held. Seligman (2006) organized a five-step process, where clients (1) learn to name the adversity that they have faced; (2) examine the beliefs that they hold about such an adversity; (3) explore the resulting consequences of holding such beliefs; (4) offer a disputation; and finally, (5) examine what Seligman calls *energization* following such disputation. Clients can learn to talk out loud, making their thoughts and beliefs automatically known. Once this happens, pessimistic beliefs can be challenged.

Seligman's (2006) makes an important caveat in his work, stressing that while "optimism is good for us" (p. 291), optimism is not necessarily something to be prescribed in all situations. In his text, he writes about the usefulness of optimism, with a specific focus on decreasing levels of depression that often results from pessimistic thinking. He suggests that optimism can be learned and used in situations when needed to move toward mental health. The goal is not blind optimism but what Seligman refers to as *flexible optimism*: "optimism with open eyes" (Seligman, 2006, p. 292).

Seligman's suggestions on intervention for optimism are in line with Antoni et al.'s (2001) suggestion that cognitive-behavioral psychological interventions may benefit clients who demonstrate low levels of optimism and that such elevations of optimism may track elevations of posttraumatic growth. However, Antoni et al. (2001) suggest that cognitive-behavioral interventions be aimed at stress management. As has been alluded to in previous chapters, when emotional stress is managed effectively, one may engage more productively in deliberate ruminations that are likely to lead to experiences of posttraumatic growth.

Turning to self-esteem and self-efficacy, the world-famous Mayo Clinic suggests a five-step cognitive-behavioral technique for boosting self-esteem:

1. Identify troubling conditions and situations
2. Become aware of beliefs and thoughts

3. Pinpoint negative or inaccurate thoughts
4. Challenge negative or inaccurate thoughts
5. Change thoughts and beliefs

It may be not only useful but also quite ethical for clinicians to engage in the aforementioned exercises themselves in addition to with their clients. In fact, if a large part of the clinical work in the field of posttraumatic growth centers on clinicians growing their personal awareness of the possibility of posttraumatic growth, then exercises that increase a clinician's ability to see growth related to optimism and self-esteem would be of benefit. It would seem to follow that the more likely therapists are to be optimistic and to have healthy levels of self-esteem, perhaps the more likely they are to be aware of growth experiences in clients' expressed narratives (though this has yet to be studied empirically).

Conclusion

Mahatma Gandhi once said, "As human beings, our greatness lies not so much in being able to remake the world—that is the myth of the atomic age—as in being able to remake ourselves." It is potentially true that we cannot change certain aspects of our personalities, such as those defined by the Five-Factor Model of personality, but there is more hope than this in life. We are not captured by our personality attributes, as Seligman professes in regard to optimism; nor are we destined to forever be held captive by our life circumstances, as the experience of great stress and trauma can lead us to momentarily believe. These two points are vitally important to remember as clinicians. Personality, just like trauma, shapes and colors our world. It may provide us with the desire to paint our sky the deepest shade of black or a brilliant hue of blue. As clinicians we are aware that clinical work is the restoration of a client's power and will to influence the color of his or her sky in a posttrauma world. This choice, freedom, and will is the remaking of the self that Gandhi preaches. Remaking a world without trauma—the one we all want to live in, and the one many of us used to live in for a time—is simply a dream, an illusion at the time, but remaking ourselves is our greatest reality. For some clients, indeed for many, such remaking includes profound experiences of previously unexperienced growth.

A Quote to Remember

Personality appears to color how people perceive life events as they take place. . . . Personality also colors perceptions along the way (DeNeve & Cooper, 1998, p. 219).

Clinical Cornerstones of the Chapter

- The Five-Factor Model of personality is thought to be related to a person's experience of well-being and, most importantly, to affect the way in which individuals react to stressful experiences (McCrae & Costa, 1986, 1991). Consequently, familiarity with this model may be quite useful for those who are interested in posttraumatic growth.
- It is suggested that personality has a modest relationship to growth, so becoming aware of the client's personality style can help better gauge any expectations the clinician may have for the possibility of posttraumatic growth.
- The personality domains of *extraversion* and *openness* appear to be most relative to growth, though evidence exists to support a connection between all five of the personality domains and growth.
- Along with the five factors, several other personality attributes are thought to be associated with growth, including optimism, self-esteem, and self-efficacy.

- Research suggests that optimism can be learned through a serious of experiences outlined by Martin Seligman (2006); further reading in this area would seem to be beneficial.
- Antoni et al. (2001) suggest that cognitive-behavioral stress management interventions may benefit clients who demonstrate low levels of optimism and that such elevations of optimism may track elevations of posttraumatic growth.
- Clients may not be able to remake *the* world, but they can remake themselves and remake *their* world. Perception is a key element in the treatment of persons who have experienced trauma.

Selected References

McCrae, R. R., & Costa, P. T. (1991). The NEO personality inventory: Using the Five-Factor Model in counseling. *Journal of Counseling & Development, 69,* 367–372.
An article by two of the leading research experts on the Five-Factor Model of personality highlighting the utility of formal assessment of personality for counselors.

DeNeve, K. M., & Cooper, H. (1998). The happy personality: A meta-analysis of 137 personality traits and subjective well-being. *Psychological Bulletin, 124,* 197–229.
This research article provides data from a meta-analysis that examined 137 personality traits, including domains of the Five-Factor Model of personality, and the relationship personality has to well-being.

Seligman, M. E. (2006). *Learned optimism: How to change your mind and your life.* New York, NY: Pocket Books.
Seligman's book outlines his argument for the ability of all people to transform their lives through cognitive-behavioral work aimed at increasing levels of optimism.

Peterson, C., Park, N., Pole N., D'Andrea, W., & Seligman, M. E. (2008). Strengths of character and posttraumatic growth. *Journal of Traumatic Stress, 21,* 214–217.

This article provides data to outline the relationship between 24 character strengths and posttraumatic growth. Various strengths assessed that are thought to have a relationship with growth include hope, bravery, perseverance, honesty, religiousness, kindness, love, creativity, curiosity, and zest.

Wiggins, J. S. (Ed.). (1996). *The Five-Factor Model of personality: Theoretical perspectives.* New York, NY: Guilford Press.

An edited work that details the history, development, and utility of the Five-Factor Model of personality. Along with the contributions of Wiggins, authors include personality psychologists Digman, Goldberg, Costa, and McCrae.

CHAPTER 7

RELATIONSHIPS

Close relationships are vitally important in our emotional and physical development as human beings. Research supports relationships between positive social support and such things as psychological well-being (Henderson & Brown, 1988), reduced levels of depression (Lara, Leader, & Klein, 1997), boosted immune functioning (Kiecolt-Glaser & Glaser, 1992), and increased resilience (Taylor, 2010). Baumeister and Leary (1995) suggest that human beings have an internal drive to be part of enduring and meaningful relationships with others. Perhaps this drive may be rooted, in part, in the idea that human beings are in many ways dependent upon their relationships with others for such things as the ability to find meaning, affirmation, protection, and connection (van der Kolk, 2006).

Relationships are important from the very first moment of our lives. The attachment literature speaks to the fundamental need for positive social relationships in our early development. For example, attachment research points to how we learn to emotionally self-regulate through the availability of our primary relationships (Bowlby, 1988; Karen, 1998). Our early relationships help shape the ways we relate to people in our adult life. If we have developed the ability to be successful in relationships with other people, and if we are fortunate to have supportive people in our inner circles as adults, then our relationships may help us to feel good, safe, and complete both physically and psychologically. With these understandings, it is perhaps not surprising that the relationships one has pre- and posttrauma are important elements in the wake of stressful and traumatic life events (Tedeschi & Calhoun, 1995, 2004).

Margaret Mead is quoted as saying, "One of the oldest human needs is having someone to wonder where you are when you don't come home at night." What is trauma but an encounter with our own personal night? The way an inner circle of family, friends, and professionals respond to one's night experience (e.g., their comfort with the discussion of stress and trauma) relates to a person's ability to move successfully through stress and trauma and their ability to potentially experience growth. In fact, supportive relationships are so vitally important in such times that even the *perception* of close relationships as being unreceptive to disclosure about stress or trauma has been found to be associated with decreased well-being (Cordova et al., 2001). Some reasons for this association may be that the perception of support from our inner circles may protect our sense of well-being by encouraging less threatening, stressful, or harmful interpretations of negative life events, by encouraging useful forms of coping, and by increasing a person's belief in his or her ability to cope successfully (Cohen, 2004).

It should not be overlooked that what we are talking about is a *perception* of support and not whether support is actually received. So then, it is not only about what our supports do that can help a person post stress and trauma, though this is of relevance as well. It is also about a belief that our supports care enough to do something (e.g., listen, encourage, feed) that is of consequence. (For those interested in more in-depth readings on the role of social support in functioning, see the listed references at the end of the chapter.)

As expressed previously, our inner circles are also responsible for actions that are useful to our sense of well-being both in times of minor and major stress. Briefly, Lepore and Revenson (2006) suggest that social support can be a useful factor in a person's experience of well-being if a relationship:

- Provides opportunities for emotional disclosure
- Allows for opportunities to process events

+ Allows for opportunities to better understand issues involved in the event
+ Provides validation of worth
+ Allows for suggestions for coping (p. 33)

One would be remiss, in a discussion of relationships, to not consider the sociocultural influence on relationships. Whether or not our relationships are available to offer such needed support may depend in part on a sense of whether the stressful or traumatic event that a person experiences is viewed as normal in one's broader and proximate cultural narrative. If one's family, friends, and community do not have previous experience with the type of stress or trauma that a person experiences, regardless of how good-natured, well-intentioned, and loving the individuals and community may be, then finding support from such relationships becomes increasingly difficult; for even close relationships may be hesitant, or uncertain as to how, to react with no cultural script to follow (Tedeschi & Calhoun, 1995). Such experiences where there is a lack of cultural script on the individual or community level narratives makes the role of the clinician and the clinical setting perhaps even more pertinent to healing and potential growth; however, the reverse is also true. As was outlined in Chapter 4, both distal and proximate cultural influences can have a positive effect on the facilitation of posttraumatic growth by allowing a person to have access to models and narratives of growth, by encouraging emotional disclosure, and by assisting a person in cognitively structuring negative life events (Calhoun, Cann, & Tedeschi, 2010).

The Role of Relationships in Models of Posttraumatic Growth

Various models of growth identify the role that social context plays in the formation of positive consequences as a result of enduring stress and trauma. Schaefer and Moos's (1998) theory on growth suggests that social support may aid in people's ability to make more positive appraisals of stress and trauma. Tedeschi and Calhoun (2006) more specifically note that close relationships with others may influence growth in several ways. Relationships may provide:

- New ways of thinking about the world
- Different ways of perceiving the world
- Additional coping methods
- Social support

Lepore and Revenson (2006) suggest that close, supportive relationships in which there is emotional disclosure may:

- Weaken connections between traumatic stimuli and negative emotional responses and in their place provide positive emotional responses
- Regulate emotions by changing the focus of attention
- Increase habituation to negative emotions
- Facilitate positive cognitive reappraisals (p. 33)

Although the suggestion of the importance of relationships is undoubtedly stressed by these researchers, more explicit details of social support are important to understand if helping professionals and the inner circle of family, friends, and communities are to be in a position to support a person who has experienced stress and trauma. Such important aspects include the type and amount of social support that facilitates growth and the potential effects that negative social support may play in the process. Research has looked into such clinically important questions and has uncovered some potentially helpful information.

Research on Social Support and Growth

Social support can be defined and measured in different and distinct ways. Types of social support include:

- Functional/tangible support
- Informational support
- Emotional support
- Quantity of support
- Level of satisfaction with support

Numerous studies have examined social support in the research literature. One example is a study by Cordova, Cunningham, Carlson, and Andrykowski (2001), in which the researchers examined posttraumatic growth following breast cancer in a controlled comparison study with a sample of 140 women: 70 women with Stage 0 to IIIB cancer who were at least 2 months posttreatment and 70 healthy women matched for age and education who did not have breast cancer. Researchers assessed a measure of social support defined as the degree to which a person felt "satisfaction with tangible and emotional support" (p. 178). Also measured in the study was a more specific aspect of social support: the degree to which a person emotionally disclosed about her cancer experience with another person or persons. The results indicated that though growth had no association with how satisfied a person was with the tangible and emotional social support she received, growth was positively associated with the degree to which a person emotional disclosed about her cancer experience with a person or persons.

A quick review of the findings may at first appear contradictory, but the study stresses that distinctive aspects of social support appear to have useful implications for growth while other aspects do not. Specifically, this study suggests that it seems less important as to whether clients express satisfaction with the support they receive—both tangible and emotional—and more important that a relationship or relationships exist with whom clients feel free and able to talk about their experiences if they should so desire it. The clinical question to consider, according to this study, is not one of the degree to which one feels satisfied with the ways close relationships in her life have responded posttrauma. Rather, the question of importance is one of whether a person feels restricted in any way by a social relationship or social relationships in regard to talking about a stress or trauma.

Similar findings were supported in a study by Weiss (2004), who examined the relationship between social support and growth in a sample of 72 married early-stage (0 to II) breast cancer survivors. Participants were diagnosis-free at the time of study, ranging from between 1 year and 5.5 years postdiagnosis. For the participants in the study, the diagnosis of cancer was their first experience with a life-threatening illness. Results indicated that a general measure of perceived social support was not related to growth, but a more specific measure of marital support (whether one's husband was perceived as supportive) was associated with more growth. In the same study, the most powerful predictor of growth was a measure of whether the sample participant had a specific person in her life who served as a role model for experiencing breast cancer and posttraumatic growth. Belief in a specific person's support was more useful to the process of growth than a general belief that people in one's life were supportive. This person need not be, and for some was not, her marital partner. In fact, in this study, what was even more beneficial to the survivor than the presence of a special person in her life who was available to discuss the stress was if that person had specific life experience that modeled struggle and growth. The results of this study are in line with Tedeschi and Calhoun's (2004) work, which suggests that the influence of available models in one's proximate and distal culture is especially useful to people who have experienced stress and trauma. Clinically, one way to assess for this beneficial aspect of culture is simply for the clinician to ask about models of posttraumatic growth among one's family or friends (Calhoun, Cann, & Tedeschi, 2010).

Further supporting the trend of the benefits of social support on growth, Schroevers, Helgeson, Sandernnan, and Ranchor (2010) examined three types of emotional social support in one study: (1) perceived social support, (2) actual social support, and (3) satisfaction with the social support that one has received. The researchers used a longitudinal research design with 206 cancer survivors from The Netherlands. Support was assessed at 3 months postdiagnosis and at 8 years postdiagnosis. Growth was also measured 8 years postdiagnosis. Results found that only actually received emotional support was associated with and predictive of posttraumatic growth. The results held true when controlling for demographics, disease-related characteristics, level of distress about the disease, and the received emotional support at 8 years postdiagnosis. The results suggest the importance of the availability of someone or some group of people to assist in the cognitive processing of traumatic events that is thought to lead to growth (Tedeschi & Calhoun, 2004; Schroevers et al., 2010). As suggested before, if such a person can serve as a model of growth with her own life, then this may be even more useful still.

It is certainly evident from the studies that growth must be understood in a sociocultural context and that loved ones in inner circles and clinicians have an important role to play in the process of posttraumatic growth. Knowing that social relationships are important, one begins to wonder:

- Just how many close relationships does a person need to facilitate growth?
- Are more friends better?
- Is there a critical number of people needed to help facilitate growth?
- Is one person enough?

Research on stress and coping not related to growth supports that one does not need a large support circle. Even the presence or perception of the presence of just one supportive person in times of stress and trauma has been found to have beneficial effects on coping (Cohen, 2004). However, research specific to growth following trauma does not yet exist to answer such questions, although preliminary evidence suggests that the number of social supports a person reports has a positive association with posttraumatic growth (Wilson & Boden, 2008).

Social support is not a one-time experience. Relationships are ongoing experiences that may change over time. Feelings of support in the wake of a traumatic event may not necessarily still be present months or years after the traumatic event, so then one must consider not merely who was in a person's life at the time of the event but who is still in a person's life months or years after the event and still serves as a provider of positive support. Perhaps equally as important is the question of who may no longer be perceived as a social support but once was able to fill that role.

Similarly, just as social support can be understood in relation to time, stress and trauma are not always acute experiences, because some stressful or traumatic events are more characteristically chronic. As mentioned earlier, research supports that social support can have a buffering effect on stress, but if the experienced stress is chronic, the buffering effect has been evidenced to disappear with time. In one study of the chronic stress of living in an overcrowded environment, researchers found that perceived social support buffered the stressful experience at 2 months after the start of the stressor, but by 8 months of enduring the stressor, the effect was no longer present (Lepore, Evans, & Schneider, 1991). Clinically then, it is important to consider the potential differences that acute and chronic stress may have on a person's circle of supports.

Anyone who has been in relationships has come to realize that not all social support is positive and that being in a relationship with some people is not always beneficial. Such nonbeneficial relationships can be considered a form of negative social support. While we need positive social relationships in our life for mental health, so too do we need a lack of negative relationships. Research suggests that not only does negative social support have a negative impact on mental health (Morgan, Neal, & Carder, 1997), but negative social interactions may be more strongly related to mental health than positive elements (Wortman, 2004). Relative to growth, Brewin's (2003) research on the relationship between social support and psychological flourishing provides support that the absence of negative or critical social interactions is at least as important as, if not more important than, the presence of positive social support in regard to growth experiences. The implication of this research is that when working with clients, assessing the absolute amount of social support may not be so important. Merely asking about the positive social support in clients' lives may not be enough. Clinically, further exploration is warranted regarding the depth of the relationship between the individual or group social support and the absence of a negative social support.

Providing Social Supports

Oprah Winfrey put it well when she noted, "Lots of people want to ride with you in the limo, but what you want is someone who will take the bus with you when the limo breaks down." There are three categories of people who may be willing to ride the bus and so provide the needed support for those who experience great stress and trauma: family/friends, other traumatized people, and professional helpers (Calhoun & Tedeschi, 1999). Each group may provide a unique role.

Some of the needed social support that a person receives actually happens before the stressful or traumatic event even occurs. "Friends and family are likely to be the only supportive others who have had an ongoing relationship with the person prior to the trauma.

Therefore, they have already played a role in preparing this person to cope with it" (Tedeschi & Calhoun, 1995, p. 95). Some examples of the ways friends and family may be helpful to a person pretrauma include:

- Early relationships that teach children to self-regulate
- Models of effective ways of coping through less stressful events
- Open relationships that encourage cognitive processing
- Relationships that validate the self
- Relationships that validate emotional disclosure
- Opportunities that promote character strengths such as optimism and creativity

Additionally, along with the beneficial role that family and friends may provide pretrauma, directly after the stressful or traumatic event, family and friends may actually serve as "mental health first responders," providing the first line of interventions that may prove to be either positive or negative support experiences. Therefore, for the clinician, understanding the client's inner circle and the numerous ways they have responded may be vitally important for successful clinical work.

Providing support can sometimes be a difficult task for family and friends. However, research concludes that beneficial growth experiences may be possible not only for the person who experienced a traumatic event, but growth can occur for family and friends who are assisting a survivor as well (Tedeschi & Calhoun, 1995). Such information may be useful to keep in mind if a clinician is also working with family members of a client.

As is well known, family and friends do not always provide social support pre- or posttrauma. In fact, in some instances, family and friends may be the least likely or available to provide support. For example, a study by Lechner et al. (2008) of individuals coping with cancer and HIV/AIDS suggested that family and friends were at times either unable or unsure how to respond to loved ones who were experiencing illness. Also, the individuals coping with illness did not always feel comfortable approaching family and friends for support. People may choose not to access support from family and friends because of a fear that they may burden their family or friends with their needs and a desire to not do this. Also, people may choose not to access support from family and friends because of a desire to protect themselves from having to respond to family and friends' potential uneasiness surrounding their illness (Lechner et al., 2008).

Research suggests that in the aforementioned scenarios, where family and friends may not be accessible, group-based interventions may be useful in fostering benefit-finding (Antoni et al., 2001; Lechner et al., 2008). For example, Antoni et al. (2001) examined the role of a 10-week cognitive-behavioral stress management intervention with a group of women diagnosed with breast cancer who had recently undergone surgery. Researchers found that in comparison to the control group who received a 1-day stress management seminar where no effect was found, women in the group intervention demonstrated increased growth at the end of the group and sustained growth after the group's end. Increased growth was related to reports of increased emotional processing of the event, which suggests that group interventions may help people process events in ways that a seminar does not.

Group-based interventions with other traumatized people may be useful in other ways as well. First, group members and group experience may be able to provide empathy for those experiencing stress and trauma, as group members understand firsthand the experience in a way loved ones may not. Second, group members may serve as role models of enduring stress and trauma in ways that lead to growth. Third, group experiences may help decrease feelings of isolation. Last, group members may offer a level of credibility to ways of enduring stress and trauma that friends, family, and clinicians simply cannot (Lechner & Antoni, 2004).

Along with family, friends, and group-based interventions, the therapist can play an important social support role as well, especially in cases when a client has limited or inadequate social relationships. For instance, a therapist can make an assessment to refer or connect the client to a group intervention if he or she believes that a client has limited or inaccessible social support from family or friends. In the absence—and even in the presence—of a supportive inner circle for clients, therapists can offer safe, confidential spaces that assist clients in cognitively processing an event. Clinicians can do this by encouraging emotional disclosure in a manner that helps clients feel safe, promotes new ways of coping, and regulates emotions.

As was mentioned earlier in the discussion of the role of sociocultural influences, a therapist may also help clients find and feel much-needed support by helping clients to identify models of support by examining the ways in which extreme stress and trauma are understood within a client's proximate and distal cultural influences. Specifically, a clinician can explore the ways in which a client's culture may influence norms about self-disclosure, barriers that may exist based on gender or the type of trauma experienced, and beliefs about the ways in which one may, or may not, be transformed by struggle (Weiss & Berger, 2010).

Finally, and perhaps most importantly, Tedeschi and Calhoun (1995) note that therapists can demonstrate a willingness to be emotionally affected by a client's story and to respond in what they consider to be the most respectful way; namely, "to listen and be touched by it" (p. 97). Such a statement suggests that one can never underestimate the healing power of being fully present with a client in a way that allows the clinician to be moved by the client's experience. This may be especially true when the story holds perhaps the darkest and most painful parts of a person's narrative to date. Listening and being touched by a trauma narrative may serve as much-needed validation that a survivor's experience (their trauma and their healing) matters not merely in the life of the survivor, but in a broader, shared narrative.

Conclusion

Growth involves nurturing intrapersonal and interpersonal experiences pre- and posttrauma (Calhoun & Tedeschi, 1999). Although a great deal of work can and must happen on the individual level, human beings are an interconnected species. We need each other. The role that a client's innermost circle of family and friends and other traumatized people play is an important one. However, in cases of great stress and trauma, support from family and friends may not be available or may not be enough. In these instances, clinicians can, and often do, play a crucial role in the healing process by offering an objective viewpoint, reliable and caring support, and by connecting clients to other resources—human and pharmacological—if warranted.

Traumatic events have a way of often leaving loved ones and even at times helping professionals wondering if there is anything they can do to help. They cannot reverse time or erase the event, but through a certain presence, a certain way of being, as was pointed out in this chapter, others can help a person who has experienced stress or trauma heal and—as the research suggests—in some instances, both the helper and the client may come to experience posttraumatic growth.

A Quote to Remember

In general, the quality of the relationships with family and friends before and after the traumatic event plays a role in determining the likelihood for growth. If good relationships can be maintained or improved, growth may be possible. (Tedeschi & Calhoun, 1995, p. 94)

Clinical Cornerstones of the Chapter

- Close relationships are vitally important in our emotional and physical development as human beings. Human beings are dependent in particular on relationships with others for such necessary things as meaning, affirmation, protection, and connection (Van der Kolk, 2006). Consequently, exploring these themes and having clients provide illustrations as to who in their interpersonal network was able to supply such supports, as well as how they were not, would be an especially useful therapeutic endeavor.

- Research supports that it may be less important that clients express satisfaction with the support that they receive—both tangible and emotional—and more important that a relationship (or several relationships) exist where a client feels able to talk freely about his or her experience and process it cognitively.

- The absolute *amount* of social support may not be so important, so asking about the positive social support in a client's life is only a first step. It is then necessary to uncover the presence of an accepting person or group of people with whom a person can talk about their experience while recognizing and assessing *the absence of a negative social support* following stressful life experiences, because this is an especially significant variable related to posttraumatic growth.

- It is helpful to remember that research suggests that people present many reasons for not disclosing to others about stress and trauma. Some may not do so because they do not want to be a burden to family or friends. Others may fear having to respond to family and friends' uneasiness with their disclosures. Because social support can be so useful, in such scenarios, group-based interventions may be useful in fostering benefit-finding (Lechner et al., 2008). Clinicians can provide the needed resources for making such referrals.

- It is helpful when therapists demonstrate authenticity and genuineness by their willingness to be emotionally affected by a client's story and to respond in the most respectful way; namely, "to listen and be touched by it" (Tedeschi & Calhoun, 1995, p. 97).

Selected References

Antoni, M. H., Lehman, J. M., Kilbourn, K. M., Boyers, A. E., Culver, J. L., Alferi, S. M., . . . & Carver, C. S. (2001). Cognitive-behavioral stress management intervention decreases the prevalence of depression and enhances benefit finding among women under treatment for early-stage breast cancer. *Health Psychology, 20,* 20–32.
A research article that stresses the importance of supportive relationships by offering evidence of a group cognitive-behavioral management intervention that resulted in an increased level of posttraumatic growth in participants.

Cohen, S. (2004). Social relationships and health. *American Psychologist, 59,* 676–684.
This article provides information for those who desire further reading on the positive role that relationships play in overall health and well-being.

Cohen, S., & Hoberman, H. (1983). Positive events and social supports as buffers of life change stress. *Journal of Applied Social Psychology, 13,* 99–125.
A useful article for those interested in further reading on the role of social support in psychological health and well-being. The article focuses on the positive benefits of social support on the experience of stress.

Tedeschi, R. G., & Calhoun, L. G. (1999). *Facilitating posttraumatic growth: A clinician's guide.* New York, NY: Routledge.
The foundational first text for clinicians that focused on the clinical aspects of posttraumatic growth, with specific attention paid to the role of social support in the process of healing and growth.

CHAPTER 8

FORGIVENESS

Fairly new exploration has begun examining the potential connections between posttraumatic growth and forgiveness. While the scientific study of forgiveness has a significant research base, the empirical study of the relationship between forgiveness and posttraumatic growth in the psychological literature is quite limited and relatively recent. It has been suggested that the relationship between the two constructs is more or less an "intuitive truth" at this point in history (Fischer, 2006), but it is also understood that even though the quantity of studies is limited, the research that does exist points to a potentially clinically important relationship between forgiveness and growth that is worthy of discussion.

Defining Forgiveness

What exactly is forgiveness? This question certainly includes some debate. One reason for such debate is that forgiveness is a construct that researchers define differently than perhaps the average person's definition of the term. The phrase "forgive and forget," for example, can lead people to link terms with forgiveness that, although they may be associated for some people, are distinct constructs. In fact, explicit attention is paid in the psychological literature to specifically separate forgiveness from such concepts as condoning, pardoning, forgetting, reconciliation, excusing, denial of harm, or restoration of a relationship (Fincham & Kashdan, 2004; Lyubomirsky, 2007; McCullough, Pargament, & Thoreson, 2000) in hopes of understanding what it really means to forgive.

McCullough et al. (2000), in a leading edited work on the theory, research, and clinical aspects of forgiveness, define forgiveness as a "prosocial change in one's motivation toward an offending partner" (p. 8). Such a definition highlights that the forgiveness, while associated with an offending partner, is not a change that necessitates any action extended toward the offending partner. The change is that of one's motivational attitude. In a similar vein, Peterson (2006) understands forgiveness as a human strength of temperance, suggesting that it articulates, in part, an action that is abstained or refrained from doing in excess rather than one additionally done (Peterson, 2006). Peterson suggests that the human strength of forgiveness protects a person from excess hatred and is evidenced in such actions as a person limiting his or her experience of anger.

What is highlighted in both understandings of the term is that though forgiveness may be associated with and/or have consequences that affect the self, another person, or (for those who are religious) a divine image, it is a change that happens both in and for the self, not for the transgressor (Lyubomirsky, 2007). In the spirit of Lewis Smedes' quotation at the opening of the chapter, although forgiving a transgressor may in some way set the transgressor free, the primary motivation of forgiveness is to set oneself free. Empirical research suggests that setting oneself free through forgiveness is beneficial to one's well-being. Particularly relevant to our discussion, forgiveness has been found to have a beneficial effect in times of stress and trauma.

For instance, Sonja Lyubomirsky (2007), in her book *The How of Happiness: A New Approach to Getting the Life You Want*, shares that as a response to normal everyday challenges in life as well as severe traumatic experiences, forgiveness has been linked to experiences of happiness. Unlike a lack of an ability to forgive, which has been found to be related to persistent negative ruminations after challenging and stressful life events, forgiving has been linked to the feeling that one is able to move on after stress and trauma of varying degrees (Lyubomirsky, 2007). This may be partly because forgiveness is a process that focuses on *releasing* one's attention to *negative* emotions after the experience of something challenging, stressful, or even traumatic and *focusing* on more *positive* ones. As was articulated in Chapter 5 in the discussion of Fredrickson's (1998, 2001) work on positive emotions, negative emotions have a tendency to constrict our thoughts and actions, whereas positive emotions have a broadening and building effect on our thoughts and actions, setting us free to play, explore, and create.

Forgiveness, Trauma, and Growth

The exchange of negative emotion for the attention of positive emotion in the process of forgiveness has led researchers to wonder about the potential relationships that may exist between forgiveness and growth after stress and trauma. Beyond merely the association, there has also been wonder about the *direction* of the relationship. Namely, does the process of forgiveness make a person more likely to grow (Fischer, 2006; Laufer, Raz-Hamama, Levine, & Solomon, 2009)? Does the process of finding benefits after stressful life events encourage forgiveness (McCullough, Root, & Cohen, 2006)? Or are both to some extent true?

In regard to the most basic question of the relatedness of forgiveness and growth, the data is somewhat conflicting. Peterson, Park, Pole, D'Andrea, and Seligman (2008), in a study of 1,739 adults, assessed several character strengths including forgiveness. After assessing for the strengths, the researchers asked participants if they had experienced any, or a number of, potentially traumatic events. Twenty-five percent of the study reported having experienced at least one of the following events:

- A life-threatening accident
- A life-threatening natural or human-made disaster

- Physical attack (including combat)
- Unwanted sexual contact under force or threat of force
- Witnessing someone being killed
- Kidnapping, captivity, or torture
- A life-threatening illness (p. 215)

The participants who indicated that they had experienced one of these events were subsequently given a measurement of posttraumatic growth. The procedures of the study are particularly interesting, because unlike many of the other studies where participants may take a measure of growth before other measures (which calls into question the potentially inflated relationships between growth and other constructs), the participants in Peterson's study were not primed to think of growth before assessing forgiveness (Peterson et al., 2008). The results of the study indicated that a significant, positive relationship existed between forgiveness and growth. The results provide preliminary evidence to suggest that the relationship between growth and forgiveness is more than just intuitive.

However, a similarly significant relationship between trauma, growth, and forgiveness was not reported in a research article by Fischer (2006), who examined the relationship in a sample of 226 individuals who were closely affected by the Oklahoma City terrorist bombings in 1995. The author highlights two important ideas in her discussion of the results that may have affected the study's findings. First, this study happened at a particularly interesting time in the United States, in that it coincidentally took place shortly after the September 2011 terrorist attacks in New York, Washington, D.C., and Pennsylvania. Such a coincidence can call into question the potential effects that the timing of the study had on the results (Fischer, 2006). Would similar results have been supported if, for example, the study took place in May of the same year, three months before the attacks, rather than in September? Did participants reexperience trauma from witnessing the event via media coverage as so many people did, or from simply hearing about the September 2001 attacks, such that it was premature to assess for growth and forgiveness in a city that had experienced a terrorist attack six years earlier?

Along with the potential effect that timing had on the study, the study also calls into question participants' personal interpretations of the word *forgiveness* (Fischer, 2006). Could research participants separate their own working definition of *forgiveness* from the psychological definition of the construct that was being examined? And if not, what effect could this have on the results? There may also be other explanations for the lack of relationship between forgiveness and growth in the Fisher study beyond the two outlined by the author. However, at the very least, we must be aware that findings of the relationship are not uniform and turn to research that helps explain the potential reasons why.

Religion's Unique Role

Although forgiveness is certainly not solely a theological notion, it does have roots as a virtue that can be found in many of the religious, spiritual, and philosophical traditions (Peterson, 2006). Therefore, researchers have turned to the potential role that religion may play in the relationship between growth and forgiveness. Specifically, researchers have begun to wonder if the level of religiosity that a person experiences could account for whether forgiveness is associated with growth (Laufer et al., 2009). A brief review of the relationship between forgiveness and several religious and spiritual traditions makes it evident why religiosity may play a role.

Take, for example, the Buddhist tradition. The Hindu Prince Siddhartha Gautama (563–483 B.C.), the founder of Buddhism, is noted for making statements such as, "To understand everything is to forgive everything" as well as "You will not be punished for your anger; you will be punished by your anger." Also in the Jewish tradition, the Torah reads, "When asked by an offender for forgiveness, one should forgive with a sincere mind and a willing spirit." From the book of common prayers in the Christian tradition as well, the Lord's Prayer reads, "Forgive us our trespasses as we forgive those who trespass against us." Also, the Prayer of St. Francis reads, "For it is in giving that we receive. It is in pardoning that we are pardoned, and it is in dying that we are born to Eternal Life."

With such examples from theology to draw upon, Laufer et al. (2009) hypothesized that forgiveness is related to growth differently for religious individuals than for nonreligious individuals. The researchers examined the potential relationship between forgiveness and posttraumatic growth in a sample of 1,482 Jewish adolescent 16-year-olds who had each been exposed to terror attacks. Three groups were examined and defined in the following ways: (1) religious (referencing adolescents who observe Jewish commandments but participate in the activities of larger society); (2) traditionalists (referencing adolescents who do not strictly adhere to religious commandments and are highly involved in the activities of the greater society), and (3) secular (referencing adolescents who do not generally practice religious commandments).

As hypothesized, results indicated that growth was experienced at different levels based on religious categories, and that forgiveness was related to growth differently based on the religious category. Growth was higher among adolescents who were part of the religious and traditional groups than those who were part of the secular group. Additionally, forgiveness was higher for adolescents in the religious group, and an unwillingness to forgive was higher for adolescents in the nonreligious groups. Finally, for adolescents in the religious group, forgiveness was associated with growth but an unwillingness to forgive was associated with nonreligious groups. The results suggest that forgiveness does have a role in growth, but this relationship may only be found in those who are religious.

More recently, Schultz, Tallman, and Altmaier (2010) examined the role of forgiveness and religion in the process of growth in a sample of 146 adults who had experienced an interpersonal transgressor. Like the previous study that examined exposure to terrorist attacks, the Schultz study included transgressors that could be considered quite significant in an individual's life. Such transgressors included experiences of sexual assault, physical harm, infidelity, theft and property damage, slander, betrayal, and lies. Results of the study indicated that the more severe and distressing the transgression in a person's life, the less forgiving a person tended to be. Also, while the total growth scale did not correlate to measures of forgiveness, one of the subscales was significantly related. Namely, the subscale of Relating to Others was positively associated with a measure of benevolence.

The researchers also found, similar to the study by Laufer et al. (2009), that religion has a role in the relationship between forgiveness and growth. Specifically, the relationship between forgiveness and growth could be accounted for by how important participants expressed their religion was to them. So then, both the Laufer et al. (2009) and the Schultz et al. (2010) studies support the clinical utility of assessing for religious and spiritual variables with clients as a means for understanding the relationship of forgiveness and growth (Schultz et al., 2010).

These studies are both correlational and cross-sectional, so it cannot be concluded from the studies if forgiveness causes growth, if growth leads to forgiveness, or if both are potentially true. The only conclusions that can be drawn are in support of a relationship that tells us that where we find high levels of forgiveness we also find high levels of growth. However, one study to date has examined the relationship between finding benefits after trauma and forgiveness in an experimental design, which allows for the examination of the direction of the relationship.

McCullough et al. (2006) examined the directional relationship between growth and forgiveness in a sample of 304 undergraduate students. In the study, participants were randomly assigned to one of three groups, in which they were directed to write about one of three assigned topics for 20 minutes: (1) traumatic aspects of an interpersonal transgression, (2) benefits of an interpersonal transgression, and (3) a control topic not related to transgressions.

Results of the McCullough et al. (2006) study indicated that people in the benefit-finding group experienced greater forgiveness toward their transgressors in comparison to participants in the other two groups. The results suggest that benefit finding may be an important component in the process of forgiveness. The authors cite research from Enright and Coyle (1998), who identified that a key aspect of forgiveness is the ability to cognitively process an event in a way that allows one to find meaning and new purpose in life (both aspects of the posttraumatic growth model) after experiencing a transgression. The authors suggest that the study provides "encouragement for efforts to integrate benefit-finding into ongoing efforts to use forgiveness as a component of clinical interventions for prevention and treatment" (p. 895). With this in mind, a few interventions that promote forgiveness are worth exploring at this point.

Interventions

Fischer (2006) writes that "therapists have a unique opportunity to offer a 'culture' of forgiveness for clients who seek help dealing with the aftermath of crisis" (p. 328). The therapist can offer a space where forgiveness is respected for the psychological benefits that many people experience as a result of changing their motivational attitude toward an offender. Yet, how does one offer such a culture of forgiveness? It would appear that some intervention is warranted posttrauma.

As is usually the case at the start of research, one can turn to case examples for preliminary evidence of successful interventions. The ability to generalize findings beyond the experience of the case is not possible, but clinical vignettes can speak to real-life examples of successful interventions. One recent article in the psychological literature, written by an anonymous author (Anonymous, 2007), serves as a case example of the usefulness of forgiveness interventions in the experience of healing and growth following a stressful and traumatic life event. The author had a unique vantage point in that he was a practicing psychotherapist as well as the driver of a motor vehicle that collided with a motorcyclist, resulting in the death of the cyclist. The author was able to witness the therapeutic effects of forgiveness interventions from both the viewpoint of a client and, in later reflection, as a therapist.

In writing of the motor vehicle accident, the author first shares the deep and profoundly negative impact that the experience had on his life, including the tremendous psychological distress he experienced. In search of a more stable psychological experience, the author shares of an intervention in which he wrote forgiveness letters to the family of the cyclist, which he sent to the family but were returned unread. He also wrote forgiveness letters to the deceased cyclist, which he kept.

In the author's experience, the writing of forgiveness letters was crucial to his processes of self-forgiveness and healing. It did not matter whether the letters were sent or received. What was critical for his healing was the action of writing the letters. (Such an understanding is expressed in the broader psychological literature on forgiveness as well.) Through the intervention of writing forgiveness letters, he was able to first express and experience a new and great appreciation for the growth he had experienced as a therapist and as a person as a result of coming to understand and accept the accident. The author's self-identified posttraumatic growth was possible partly because of the processing of the experience of the accident in his life through the forgiveness writing intervention. In his own words, he shares, "I gained insights as a psychotherapist through my accident experience that I might not have been able to obtain any other way" (p. 561). He shares as well:

> Writing such letters reduces shame and guilt, potentially opens up lines of communication in the case of admitting to one's mistakes, or results in greater compassion and perspective in instances of forgiving others for ways in which one was hurt or betrayed. (p. 564)

Letter writing can happen in private, but letters can also be completed in the presence of and with the help of people in one's support circle. For the author, what proved to be most fruitful and healing was writing forgiveness letters with the guidance and support of his family, friends, and a therapist.

It is too early in the research to offer information conclusively on whether forgiveness interventions, such as the letter writing intervention, are specifically helpful relative to facilitating growth posttrauma. However, research supports how one could encourage and strengthen the virtue of forgiveness in clients and in the clinician's life too if it is deemed to be clinically and personally useful.

Peterson (2006) suggests three specific ways to strengthen forgiveness that can be completed in private or with the guidance of a therapist:

1. Let a grudge go every day.
2. When you feel annoyed, even with justification, take the high road and do not tell anyone how you feel.
3. Write a forgiveness letter; do not send it, but read it every day for a week. (p. 160)

Similarly, Lyubomirsky (2007) suggests the following strategies for practicing forgiveness that can be performed in journal, letter, or conversation forms. These interventions can also be completed privately or in the presence of a therapist:

- Appreciate being forgiven.
- Imagine forgiveness.
- Write a letter of forgiveness.
- Practice empathy.
- Consider charitable attributions about the transgressor.
- Ruminate less.
- Make contact (not necessarily literally).
- Remind yourself about forgiveness.

Such practices do not take much time, but if incorporated into one's daily life, they may help encourage a culture of forgiveness in the individual who performs them, whether a client or clinician.

A proviso, though, is in order here: It seems important to note that current thinking is that one must make an individual assessment and determination *pre*intervention of the potentially negative consequences that may accompany forgiveness exercises before encouraging forgiveness interventions (Fincham & Kashdan, 2004). In some cases, forgiveness may be counterproductive to both healing and growth. Clinically, we also need to ensure that forgiveness is not explored because it is in the interest of the client's family, friends, religious community, or even the clinician. The point is that there is enough evidence to support openness to the possibility of a forgiveness intervention that should be entertained by the client and therapist, but forgiveness interventions should not necessarily be encouraged universally.

At this point, the relationship between forgiveness and growth is still exploratory, with only a handful of studies examining the relationship. The research seems to suggest that while forgiveness may not be necessary for posttraumatic growth (Fischer, 2006), for some populations, such as the religious, it may be a core factor in the process. It seems that work can be done pretrauma to encourage more forgiveness in an individual, be that individual client or clinician. Such work appears necessary to consider, especially because the current popular American culture has a tendency to value character traits that are quite distant from forgiveness (Lyubomirsky, 2007). If forgiveness interventions are deemed to be clinically useful, then the culture that a therapist can offer in a clinical setting need not value the same distance from forgiveness that is often seen in American culture.

A Quote to Remember

As therapists, our goal is to help individuals who experience purposeful acts of terror or violence not only to reduce the distressing emotions that accompany these experiences, but also to return to a life of meaning and purpose. The act of forgiveness offers the possibility of a new beginning from injuries of the past. Posttraumatic growth offers us a way to understand a newfound appreciation for life and psychological strength that may result from coping with past trauma. A therapist's understanding and facilitation of both forgiveness and posttraumatic growth can offer hope and healing not otherwise available to our clients (Fischer, 2006, p. 327).

Clinical Cornerstones of the Chapter

- At this point, the relationship between forgiveness and growth is still exploratory. Yet, studies provide preliminary evidence for the use of forgiveness as a component of clinical interventions for prevention and treatment of stressful and traumatic events.
- For clients who have experienced stressful and traumatic events, therapists have a unique opportunity to provide a culture of forgiveness (Fischer, 2006) in a way that the American culture in general does not.

+ Individual assessment and determination must be made before encouraging forgiveness interventions in order to consider the potential for negative consequences of such exercises; in some instances, forgiveness should not be encouraged but openness to it explored and considered at the *right juncture for the client.* As was mentioned, care should be taken that action regarding forgiveness is not being taken because of others' needs.

Selected References

Anonymous (2007). The impact that changed my life. *Professional Psychology: Research and Practice, 38,* 561–570.

This article recounts the experience of the author as the driver of a car that collided with a motorcycle and resulted in the death of the cyclist. The article shares the author's experience as a client, the specific role that forgiveness played in his healing and growth, and the lessons he learned as a clinician working in the area of trauma, healing, forgiveness, and growth.

Fischer, P. C. (2006). The link between posttraumatic growth and forgiveness: An intuitive truth. In L. G. Calhoun & R. G. Tedeschi (Eds.), *Handbook of posttraumatic growth: Research and practice (pp. 311–333).* Mahwah, NJ: Erlbaum.

A chapter in Calhoun and Tedeschi's edited text, which outlines research the author conducted with people personally affected by the Oklahoma City bombing of 1995. The research article provides evidence for the lack of a relationship between forgiveness and growth and points to several possible explanations for this lack of a relationship.

McCullough, M. E., Pargament, K. I., & Thoresen, C. (Eds.). (2000). *Forgiveness: Theory, research, and practice.* New York, NY: Guilford Press.

An edited work on the psychological construct of forgiveness. Chapters include a comprehensive overview of the construct, including information on the history, meanings/definition, measurement, assessment, relationships to health, neuropsychological correlates, personality, and therapeutic interventions.

McCullough, M. E., Root, L. M., & Cohen A. D. (2006). Writing about the benefits of an interpersonal transgression facilitates forgiveness. *Journal of Consulting and Clinical Psychology, 74,* 887–897.

This article provides empirical evidence of an experimentally designed study to facilitate forgiveness.

CHAPTER 9

FAITH, SUFFERING, AND RELIGIOUS COPING

Mental health can provide understandings of the processes and outcomes of stress and trauma, but in regard to the question of why stress and trauma exist in the life of the person sitting across from the therapist, the silence can be deafening at times. Religion, on the other hand, perhaps more than any other discipline, is routinely called on to respond to the philosophical and religious questions that are raised by the existence of suffering in our world and in our lives (Bemporad, 2005). Moreover, one can gather from understanding the theological conversations on suffering that what the posttraumatic growth literature is saying—namely, that struggle can lead to paradoxical beneficial outcomes—is not new.

An understanding of the foundational tenets of various religious perspectives can be helpful to clinicians who work with religious or spiritual persons. This is a delicate process. Clinicians need to be open to those clients who are encouraged by continuing to live by the tenets of their faith and who are able to access coping mechanisms, rituals, and metaphors embedded in their religious traditions that may be useful in their efforts toward healing, yet care needs to be taken not to take a personal stand. Consequently, whenever possible, *as in the case of any multicultural situation*, an understanding of the faith traditions of clients may allow a clinician deeper insight into any tension that may exist between how clients experience the world and how they perceive that their faith tradition tells them they ought to do so.

From experience and research, we also know, as might be expected, that religion and spirituality may be a source of great distress; trauma is an experience that can threaten, harm, or even alter a person's spiritual beliefs as well (Falsetti, Resick, & Davis, 2003). It is no surprise that understanding religious and spiritual themes may allow clinicians access to information that could inform interventions in ways that a lack of awareness might prevent. Recent scientific evidence implies how understanding the ways in which clients integrate religion and spirituality into their lives can then be clinically significant when working with stress and trauma. As a matter of fact, research on the psychology of religion, spiritual aspects of psychotherapy, and pastoral counseling point out that religion and spirituality can tell clinicians something more about clients' well-being than personality variables explain alone (Piedmont, 2005).

Confronting suffering is a central function of religion, so people frequently look to faith for help and support in difficult times (Hauser, 1994). An examination of the theological literature reveals that the foundation of the psychological process of posttraumatic growth can be seen in theological beliefs from various religious traditions (Calhoun & Tedeschi, 2006). One Western tradition (Christianity) will be highlighted as a means of providing evidence for such a statement; however, the use of Christianity in this chapter is not meant to imply that it is the only or the primary faith tradition where connections can be seen. The wisdom of an Eastern atheistic tradition—Buddhism—will also be discussed further in the Epilogue. Indeed, it seems that all faith traditions address the connections between suffering and growth in some way. In offering this perspective of one faith tradition, the intent is to encourage readers to also delve further on their own into how suffering is viewed in such major faith orientations as Buddhism, Judaism, Islam, and Hinduism, among others.

Christian Perspectives on Suffering and Growth

Christianity provides a framework for viewing suffering as paradoxical. People of the Christian faith believe that enduring suffering can lead to a deeper, more authentic relationship with God (Lewis, 1961) and to the development of character virtues (Roberts, 2007). The main religious text of the Christian faith tradition, the Bible (which includes the Old Testament/Hebrew Scripture and the New Testament), offers several examples of such connections between suffering and growth. In the Hebrew Scripture, the Book of Job, for instance, serves as a prime example of the relationship that humankind can have with suffering. The story attests to the lack of a quid pro quo relationship between human suffering and God. It provides an example of a man whose faith was challenged repeatedly but not lost through trauma. In the end, Job makes a proclamation in the Hebrew scriptures that emphasizes a choice in a relationship with the Divine as a means of enduring his struggle: "I know my redeemer lives" (Job 19:25). Such a statement serves as an example of how faith can be strengthened, not thwarted, by the coexistence of the experience of suffering and a belief in God. Such a statement also is further developed in the New Testament and exemplifies the Christian belief in a loving, savior image of a God who can and does coexist with an image of a God who allows suffering (Cataldo, 2008).

In the New Testament, the connection between suffering and growth can be seen in the story of Jesus. The life, death, and resurrection story provides believers with a transcendent view of suffering. The suffering experienced in this world is placed within a temporary context, and so suffering in essence loses some of its cognitive grip on a person. The story also provides an example of how suffering and love can coexist; how even the most tremendous experiences of suffering can be met with faith, patience, trust, and love (Hauser, 1994). The Christian New Testament stories understand joy and pain not as exclusive (Harrington, 2000) but rather as experiences that may occur simultaneously.

The Christian faith speaks of how the act of enduring suffering demands that people increase their confidence in the power of God to sustain them (Hauser, 1994). The confidence needed in the power of God when one is not suffering is less than the confidence needed in God when one is suffering. The Christian writer C. S. Lewis captured his struggle to find his "Christian God," which is related in his book, *A Grief Observed.* In it, he describes the deep pain he experienced when he was faced with the death of a loved one. He wrote:

> You never know how much you really believe anything until it is a matter of life and death to you. It is easy to say you believe a rope to be strong and sound as long as you are merely using it to cord a box. But suppose you had to hang by the rope over a precipice. Wouldn't you then first discover how much you really trusted it? (Lewis, 1961, p. 34)

From a Christian orientation, and in the case of several other faith traditions that are theistic (in contrast to Buddhism, for instance, which is atheistic and does not have a personal god concept), suffering allows people to reveal the degree to which they possess authentic faith in God and invites people to strengthen their faith in a way that other experiences do not. Like a magnifying glass, it enlarges the questions of how people have come to understand themselves, their god, and the relationship between the two.

The construal of human suffering from a Christian faith perspective provides significance to the experience. Suffering is not isolated and pointless. Suffering, like all life events, is construed in terms of one's relationship to Jesus (Roberts, 2007). Suffering is a meaning-filled component that can be grist for the mill of living the spiritual life if people's religious convictions are able to integrate it (Hauser, 1994). If integrated in a mature way, faith can construe the emotional experience of suffering as a useful way to acknowledge and deepen their personal relationship with God. People may, for example, come to realize that they are in a privileged context (Harrington, 2000), sharing parallel experiences with their god. From a Christian perspective, they may find more meaning in personal relationships and more purpose in life by feeling a deeper connection with God.

Take, for example, Joan, a 55-year-old woman who lost her daughter, Sara, to leukemia at the age of 7. Joan shares the following:

> Losing my child is undoubtedly the most difficult experience of my life. Sara was filled with so much light, so much joy. She had an enthusiastic love for people. Even in the hospital, through all the treatments, all the pain, she oozed love for the other children, for the medical staff, for so many people, many of whom I could not imagine loving. But there was one moment, in the last week of her life, where Sara was so tired, so sad, and she started to cry. Not an intense sob, it was weeping. I took her in my arms, and she said to me softly, "Mommy, I don't want to leave you and Daddy alone. I don't want you to be sad." Losing Sara has led me to understand my faith in a new way. I wonder about things that I took for granted in my faith before. The passage in the Bible that recollects how Jesus wept at his cruxification. I must have heard it in church forty times. But it means something different now. My faith, my God, means something different now.

An attempt at explaining the paradox created between the idea of suffering as intrinsic to the human condition within the same story that speaks of a powerful god who cares for creation is examined as the mystery of *theodicy* (why a god who is supposed to be good allows suffering). In looking at theodicy, Christian theologians have sought to find reconciliation between the two seeming contradictions. The Soul-Building Theodicy, based on the works of

Thomas Aquinas (1945), makes the reconciliation of evil and suffering in a world with a loving God by indicating that some goods can only grow in a world where evil exists, and that one example of such goods are those virtues that one practices through suffering (Hall & Johnson, 2001). So then while human suffering can slam its victims against a solid wall of evil, according to certain Christian apologists, so too can it also transform its victims into some of the most beautiful of human persons (Liderbach, 1992). From this point of view, the Christian faith does not seek struggle, but it acknowledges that it exists and so uses it, as it does all else, to form a deeper relationship with God through the self and with God through others. In this faith tradition, it is interesting that just as in the scientific process of posttraumatic growth, the trauma, the stress, and the suffering are allowed to remain intrinsically negative while also allowed to be the fulcrum and impetus for new, possibly amazing, growth.

Take the words of Desmond Tutu, the first black South African Anglican Archbishop of Cape Town and a Nobel Peace Prize Winner for his physical and verbal presence in the fight against the trauma created by apartheid and other various forms of oppression. He writes:

> Dear Child of God,
>
> I write these words because we all experience sadness, we all come at times to despair, and we all lose hope that the suffering in our lives and in the world will ever end. I want to share with you my faith and my understanding that this suffering can be transformed and redeemed. There is no such thing as a totally hopeless case. Our God is an expert at dealing with chaos, with brokenness, with all the worst that we can imagine.
>
> God created order out of disorder, cosmos out of chaos, and God can do so always, can do so now—in our personal lives and in our lives as nations, globally. The most unlikely

person, the most improbable situation—these are all "trans-figurable"—they can be turned into their glorious opposites. Indeed, God is transforming the world now—through us—because God loves us. (Tutu, 2004, p. vii)

Although Tutu's words are from a Christian perspective, it is interesting to note that they are also very much in tune with many of the premises and findings from studies on posttraumatic growth. Many well-known Christian leaders who have undergone suffering themselves would proclaim at certain advanced stages of their response to it: Transformation is not only possible, it is happening all around us, in our minds, hearts, and world. The world, which is filled with suffering, is all transfigurable. For each suffering that is born, there too is born a hope. In speaking to clinicians and reviewing qualitative studies, some of the narratives from survivors of abuse and other types of trauma or serious stress echo Tutu's observations.

Interestingly, it has been proposed that the very developmental foundation of the Christian church can be conceptualized as a posttraumatic growth experience as well. McGrath (2006) explains that the church existed with a predeath schema of the world. The Christian church then experienced the traumatic death of its leader, which resulted in great distress. The collective church engaged in a new meaning-making process, searching for the comprehensibility and significance of the event. Rumination about the death of Jesus took place and eventually led to the experience of paradoxical wisdom of a Messiah who was both a human sufferer and savior, thus transforming suffering for Christians and laying the foundation for a theology of hope based on the resurrection. The implication of McGrath's work is a widening and deepening of the connections of Christian faith tradition to posttraumatic growth. For it is not only the *content* of the Christian religious texts and contemporary writers that exemplifies growth, it is actually the very *process* of the development of the church.

Recent Relevant Research

Data suggests that religious and spiritual beliefs are common in the general population. In fact, according to the Princeton Religious Research Center (1990s), 96% of adults in the United States express a belief in God. Data also suggests that people call on their faith in times of stress and trauma, in many different ways. The significant elements that both researchers and clinicians now realize and are looking at more deeply related to faith are that it is a:

+ Meaning-making system
+ Form of coping
+ Way of orienting to selves and the world

For instance, Pargament, Desai, and McConnell (2006) suggest that in difficult times three critical growth-related aspects of faith are that (1) they can play a critical role in meaning-making; (2) they can offer support and empowerment; and (3) they can foster life-changing transformations of personal priorities and goals. A review of the literature indicates further that posttraumatic growth and these aspects of religion and spirituality are consistently associated (Linley & Joseph, 2004).

Faith as a Framework for Meaning

Research suggests that religious and spiritual beliefs have a central role in the meaning-making process and in rebuilding founda-tional life assumptions that are threatened or shattered by trauma (Matthews & Marwit, 2006). As was articulated in Chapter 3, the importance of finding meaning after experiencing stress and trauma is essential. For many people, faith provides a unique framework for making sense of difficult times. In fact, it has been suggested that a religious belief system is perhaps the most unfailing way to make meaning from injustice, suffering, and trauma (Park, 2005a). Religion and spiritual belief systems can provide a framework for how to emotionally construe events. When faced with a stressful or traumatic life event that human beings cannot explain, religion and spirituality may be able to provide individuals with an answer that other nonreligious forms of coping cannot (Pargament & Park, 1997).

The relationship between faith and meaning has been evidenced in several studies. For example, in a sample of 124 parents whose children died of Sudden Infant Death Syndrome (SIDS), greater religious participation was associated with a parent's ability to find a sense of meaning in the loss of their child (McIntosh, Silver, & Wortman, 1993). Likewise, in a sample of 457 male and female graduate and undergraduate students affected by the September 2001 terrorist attacks, spiritual meaning was related to both lower levels of depression and anxiety (Ai, Cascio, Santangelo, & Evans-Campball, 2005). The relationship between meaning and religion lays a foundation for understanding how faith may be used in the meaning-making process (Park & Folkman, 1997) and posttraumatic growth in general (Park, 2005a).

Park (2005a) examined the relationship among faith, meaning, and posttraumatic growth. In a sample of 169 male and female undergraduate students who reported they had experienced a significant death in the previous year, religion correlated positively with meaning-making coping, stress-related growth (a term synonymous with posttraumatic growth), and well-being. The association indicates that where meaning-making coping is found, religion and growth is usually also found. The study revealed that the relationship between religion and stress-related growth was partially mediated by meaning-making coping, suggesting that a significant part (but not all) of the relationship between religion and growth can be accounted for by the relationship between religion and meaning. Religion, it appears from this study, is one way that people find meaning and thus grow following stress. The clinical implication of such a study is that it may be useful to gather information about clients' religious or spiritual beliefs and how they may be using information in their search to make meaning after stressful life experiences. What is of question clinically is not which of the organized faith traditions clients belong to (though knowledge of such a faith tradition is clinically useful information for a clinician to have), but rather how clients experience or access their own particular faith tradition as a source of meaning.

Religious/Spiritual Practices and Participation

Engaging in religious and spiritual practices is one way in which many people develop beliefs about meaning and purpose in the world (Weaver et al., 2003). Posttraumatic growth has been linked to religious and spiritual practices in several studies. In one sample of 174 male and female bereaved HIV/AIDS caregivers, Cadell et al. (2003) found that individuals who engage in more spiritual practices experience more posttraumatic growth.

Several different behaviors fall under the category of religious and spiritual practices and participation. One of the more common spiritual practices (with research showing a connection to posttraumatic growth) is prayer. Studies report varying ranges of Americans who pray. Percentages have been reported as low as 30% in a general social survey (Shahabi et al., 2002) and as high as 80% in a sample of older adults admitted to a hospital for a medical illness (Koenig, 2004).

When and why people pray may vary depending on their level of stress and even the type of stress. Prayer may be a particularly useful form of coping for illness-related stresses and traumas, because unlike other forms of coping that require a certain degree of physical health (e.g., exercise, gardening, visiting with friends), prayer is something that does not require any degree of health

(Koenig, 2010). Sight, hearing, and mobility can completely fail a person, but prayer remains accessible.

There is evidence of a relationship between prayer and posttraumatic growth. In a sample of 175 women breast cancer survivors, Levine, Aviv, Yoo, Ewing, and Au (2009) reported that 81% of the sample prayed, and these women scored significantly higher on the measure of posttraumatic growth than women who reportedly did not pray. The results suggest that women who pray find more positive outcomes of their breast cancer experience than women who do not pray. If prayer is understood to be a form of "communication with God" (Meraviglia, 2006, p. E3), then one possible conclusion of the results is that a mature relationship with a person's god brings a sense of faith and assurance during stressful life experiences that aids in the process of posttraumatic growth. Conversely, the lack of assurance and faith an individual has in his or her relationship with god may have deleterious effects on post-traumatic growth.

A study by Harris et al. (2008) also examined the relationship between prayer and posttraumatic growth, taking into account not merely *if* sample participants prayed, but rather *why* they prayed. In a sample of 327 churchgoing, self-identified trauma survivors, prayer was assessed using the four coping functions identified by Bade and Cook (2008): (1) prayer as actively seeking help, (2) prayer as seeking to increase one's ability to accept the stressor, (3) prayer as seeking to help focus coping efforts, and (4) prayer as deferring or avoiding the stressor. Results indicated that posttraumatic growth was positively associated with all forms of prayer. Implications suggest then that prayer can be performed in a variety of ways that lead to growth.

It appears from the studies that a positive relationship exists between meaning that can be formulated from faith traditions, spiritual practices, and the growth experienced following stressful and traumatic circumstances. It should also be noted that the relationship among faith, meaning, and posttraumatic growth leaves open many questions yet to be determined by researchers. For example, what if any influence is there on the relationship between posttraumatic growth and the type of prayer (e.g., petitionary, intercessory)? Is prayer relative to the religious orientation of a person? Furthermore, because the religious and spiritual practices that a person engages in are only one aspect of faith that is relative to struggle and growth, how does the research on prayer fit into other relationships that exist between aspects of people's religion/spirituality and their level of growth following trauma?

Religious Coping

The research on religious coping reveals that the relationship between religious and spiritual variables and posttraumatic growth is more complex than studies on other aspects of faith. Religious coping is a multidimensional variable that takes into account an understanding that in some instances religion and spirituality can aid a person in experiencing levels of posttraumatic growth, whereas in other instances religion and spirituality can serve as a means of additional distress in an already difficult time.

Religious coping is conceptualized as having two higher-order patterns (Pargament et al., 1998). A *positive* religious coping pattern is understood as a form of coping that expresses "a secure relationship with God, a belief that there is a greater meaning to be found in life, and a sense of spiritual connectedness with others" (Pargament et al., 2001, p. 498). A *negative* religious coping pattern is understood as a form of coping that expresses "a less secure relationship with God, a tenuous and ominous view of the world, and a religious struggle to find and conserve significance in life" (Pargament et al., 2001, p. 498). A meta-analysis on religious coping and stress also reveals (perhaps not surprisingly) that positive religious coping has a positive association with psychological adjustment and a negative association with negative psychological adjustment. Additionally, negative religious coping appears to have a positive association with negative psychological adjustment and a negative association with positive psychological outcomes (Ano & Vasconcelles, 2005). Although posttraumatic growth is a concept understood as distinct from adjustment, the research on religious coping and posttraumatic growth, in general, shares a similar pattern to that of adjustment.

The relationship between positive and negative religious coping and posttraumatic growth has been examined by many researchers. For example, in a fairly recent study, Proffitt et al. (2007) examined a sample of 30 religious clergy and ordained ministers and found that high levels of positive religious coping were related to high levels of growth, and high levels of negative religious coping were related to low levels of growth.

Pargament et al. (2004) also examined the relationship between positive and negative religious coping and posttraumatic growth in a sample of 268 medically ill elderly patients in a 2-year longitudinal study. Both positive and negative religious coping at the start of the study were able to predict changes in posttraumatic growth over time. A post hoc examination of negative religious coping over time revealed that participants who scored high on the measure of negative religious coping at both the start of the study *and* 2 years later had reported significant declines in quality of life, depressed mood, and functional status. The results suggest that negative religious coping is an important variable to consider when working with posttraumatic growth, and one that does not just improve or go away with the passage of time. Another interesting result of this study—separate from the results on coping—was that regardless of whether a person's illnesses took a turn for the better or for the worse, growth was still evidenced. It appears from this study that one does not need to overcome an illness to experience growth.

Further support for the relationship between posttraumatic growth and religious coping is evidenced by Pargament et al. (1998) in three studies using diverse samples. The three samples included: (a) 296 male and female members of two churches in Oklahoma at the time of the terrorist bombing of a federal building, (b) 540 male and female college students who experienced a serious negative event during the 3 years before the study, and (c) 551 male and female medically ill patients over the age of 55. In all three samples, posttraumatic growth consistently correlated with positive religious coping and with negative religious coping.

Koenig, Pargament, and Nielsen (1998) examined more specific aspects of the relationship between religious coping, posttraumatic growth, and psychological functioning in a large sample of 577 medically ill patients age 55 or older. Results found that the negative religious coping behaviors of seeing illness as punishment from God, reprisals involving demonic forces, pleading for direct intercession, and expression of spiritual discontent were all related to significantly poorer physical health, worse quality of life, and greater depression. In the literature, these facets of negative religious coping are called "spiritual struggle" and have consistently been found to be related to poorer mental health and physical health (Pargament et al., 2004). It has also been suggested that spiritual struggles can exacerbate distress (Ano & Vasconcelles, 2005) and even predict mortality (Oxman et al., 1995; Pargament et al., 2004).

Clinically, spiritual struggles may be an obstacle to the experience of growth. Clinicians may need to assess for, and address, spiritual struggles when working with people experiencing stressful life events. Although religiousness may be helpful in buffering stress (Hood et al., 1996), it is clear from the studies that not everyone experiences religion and spirituality in the same way. *Sometimes* the ways people use religion might be harmful for *some* individuals (Murphy et al., 2000), so the unique ways that people use faith to cope as it relates to stress and trauma must be recognized by the clinician.

Religious Orientation

Religious orientation is the approach that one takes toward religion (Allport & Ross, 1967). Foundational research on religious orientation considered two different ways of orienting oneself: *extrinsic* (religion for the sake of something else—social outlets, coping, etc.) and *intrinsic* (religion for the sake of religion). It has been proposed that intrinsic religiosity is the basis of a mature faith (Allport & Ross, 1967). Since the foundational research, religious orientation has been used in numerous studies of psychological functioning. In addition, the measures of the variable itself have expanded. Religious orientation is relative to posttraumatic growth in that it is the variable that addresses the ways one faith tradition manifests differently from one person to the next. Knowing that religion is individual is key in that it brings one closer to understanding why for some people faith can assist in growth and for others it does not.

Calhoun et al. (2000) examined the extent to which religious orientation predicted posttraumatic growth. Religious orientation was measured with the Quest Scale (Batson, Schoenrade, & Ventis, 1993), a measure of the degree to which a person's religion involves a "responsive dialogue with existential questions" (Batson et al., 1993, p. 169). The Quest Scale includes three subscales: Openness (openness to religious change), Readiness (readiness to face existential questions), and Doubt (self-criticism and perception of religious doubt as positive). In the sample of 54 male and female students who had experienced a major traumatic event in the 3 years before the study, it was found that growth correlated positively to the Quest subscale of Readiness. The implication of such a relationship being: Where one finds high levels of readiness to face existential questions in life, one also finds high levels of posttraumatic growth. Given this finding, it seems as though certain religious orientations may serve as a primer of sorts for the work of traumatic growth, which necessitates a review of existential, often irreconcilable life events. There are obvious clinical implications for the need to understand the way people approach their faith. A limitation of this study is the small sample size, as it calls into question the power of the study or the ability to see statistical relationships if they exist. Therefore, although there is evidence for the role of religious orientation and posttraumatic growth, the extent and degree of the relationship may have been underscored or even missed.

More recently, Wilson and Boden (2008) examined the relationship between posttraumatic growth and religious orientation in an Australian sample. The researchers tested a model in which religious orientation and social support served as mediators of (or the link between) the relationship between posttraumatic growth and personality. The sample consisted of 104 predominantly female participants from Australia. Researchers found that posttraumatic growth significantly correlated with religious orientation and religious attitude. The results also indicated that religious orientation could predict posttraumatic growth. The clinical implication of these research studies is that assessing the religious orientation and meaning for the client could be useful in therapy.

Final Comments

The relationship between faith and posttraumatic growth is exciting, because it is complex and a potentially powerful factor in treatment. Understanding that a client belongs to a certain faith tradition is only the beginning of understanding how the faith tradition may already greatly influence the client's search for meaning, support, empowerment, purpose, and—most ideally—health. Given this potential, this chapter has sought to provide an example of how the relationship between struggle and growth in the posttraumatic growth literature intersects with various faith stories, provides information on the current research in the area, and offers insight into the way that research can inform clinical practice. It should be noted that at times the work of integrating religious and spiritual themes may begin to feel outside the realm of the therapeutic role or stance. At these times, it is important for clinicians to seek consultation not only with colleagues but also with spiritual leaders in the client's faith tradition for the good of the client, for the good of therapy, and—with respect to the particular interest here—for the good of possible growth following the experience of trauma.

A Quote to Remember

For people experiencing injustice, suffering, or trauma, a religious belief system and its associated goals may be the most unfailing way to make meaning from their experience. (Park, 2005b, p. 304)

Clinical Cornerstones of the Chapter

- Religion and spirituality have both positive and negative associations with posttraumatic growth. Knowing this makes the counselor sensitive to a potentially important area impacting posttraumatic growth.
- The real question clinically goes beyond *what* organized faith clients belong to, but more importantly *how* clients experience or access their faith. Consequently, the clinician must be prepared to explore this area if and when it comes up in treatment.
- Sight, hearing, or mobility can completely fail; yet, prayer as a coping mechanism is still accessible and within reach for many clients. If they mention that they are people of prayer, discussing what their faith tradition teaches about how to pray and whether they have mentors from their tradition to support them would seem to be a culturally sensitive step to take.

+ As with all cultural aspects, not everyone uses religion and spirituality in the same way. Sometimes the ways people use religion might be harmful. In those cases, the clinician (while taking care not to interfere with people's faith tradition) can and should question how they are accessing what they believe.
+ Certain religious orientations (e.g., quest-seeking) may serve as an aide to the work of traumatic growth, which necessitates a review of existential, often irreconcilable life events. Accordingly, any knowledge of existential psychology, as well as the spiritual quest approaches of different faith traditions, adds to the counselor's multicultural awareness.
+ Conducting a spiritual assessment at some point in the clinical session may be helpful. For this to be undertaken, consultation with faith leaders and with therapists who are trained in working with religiously committed clients, as well as with religious and spiritual themes in counseling, may become necessary in certain cases. Certain psychometric spiritual assessment tools (i.e., the Assessment of Religious and Spiritual Sentiments [ASPIRES, Piedmont, 2004]) may also be helpful in this regard.

Selected References

Matthews, L. T., & Marwit, S. J. (2006). Meaning reconstruction in the context of religious coping: Rebuilding the shattered assumptive world. *Omega, 53*, 87–104.
    This article provides a review of and clarification on the relationships among the concepts of meaning reconstruction, shattered assumptions, and religious coping.
Pargament, K. I., & Park, C. L. (1997). In times of stress: The religion-coping connection. In B. Spilka & D. McIntosh (Eds.), *The psychology of religion: Theoretical approaches* (pp. 43–53). Boulder, CO: Westview Press.

A chapter in an edited text that provides an overview of the relationship among religion, coping, and stress.

Park, C. L. (2005a). Religion as a meaning-making framework in coping with life stress. *Journal of Social Issues, 61*, 707–729.
This paper presents data from primary research to support a relationship between religion and meaning-making coping.

Park, C. L. (2005b). Religion and meaning. In R. Paloutzain & C. L. Park (Eds.), *Handbook of psychology and religion* (pp. 295–313). New York, NY: Guilford Press.
A chapter in an edited text provides an overview of the relationship between religion and meaning, citing numerous studies.

Tutu, D. (2004). *God has a dream: A vision of hope for our time*. New York, NY: Doubleday.
This is a theological reflection on suffering and hope within the context of racial oppression from the perspective of an Anglican priest.

Weaver, A. J., Flannelly, L. D., Garbarino, J. K., Figley, C. R., & Flannely, K. J. (2003). A systematic review of research on religion and spirituality in the *Journal of Traumatic Stress*: 1990–1999. *Mental Health, Religion, & Culture, 6*, 215–228.
This article provides a broad review of a decade of research on the relationship among religion, spirituality, and its role in coping with stress.

On the Road to Wisdom:
Being a Mindful
Companion on the Path to
Posttraumatic Growth

An Epilogue

Even though trauma and dramatic personal darkness are relatively rare, everyone experiences personal darkness in various forms at different times in life. Abuse, war, serious rejection, tragic loss, deep sadness, profound physical illness, caring for a parent with Alzheimer's, unexpected divorce, unwanted dramatic changes at work, and other forms of trauma and serious stress are encountered by many of the people who come to us—as well as, of course, by us at times. Unfortunately, they are part of life.

Although such trauma and stress are certainly undesirable, as we have seen, they can take people to places in themselves and life they have never encountered before *if* they have the wherewithal to see and embrace the promise such experiences offer. With this in mind, the question discussed from several angles in this book has been: What does it take for people to respond to significant stress and trauma in ways that deepen and possibly make them more compassionate? Or will these negative events fail to provide any benefit and lead only to numbness and bitterness or, at best, return them to a premorbid level of functioning?

Almost in response to this very question, two movements have occurred in the behavioral sciences. One, *positive psychology*, has given life to an area being referred to now as *posttraumatic growth*, which points to the ways suffering can lead to amazingly fortunate results. The other, *mindfulness* (being open and fully "in the now"), based on Buddhist psychology, has been put forth by several schools of thought (including Cognitive-Behavioral Therapy and Acceptance and Commitment Therapy) as a way of becoming present in order to diminish anxiety and enhance the quality of life.

These two psychological advances are even more fascinating because they build on each other, as well as provide empirical evidence and new angles of vision, with respect to the classic and contemporary wisdom literature from philosophy, spirituality, and humanistic-existential psychology that predated them. In the past, as most will now acknowledge, clinical psychology was so pathology-driven and in line with the medical model that it viewed the challenges people faced in life as acute. In other words, the goal was to find out what was causing the problem, fix it, and then move on (although as Brazier [1995] recognized in his important work *Zen Therapy*, it was often a return to what Freud referred to as a stage of "ordinary unhappiness").

The literature from existentialists, a nontheistic approach such as Zen Buddhism, and other world spiritualities though had a seemingly opposite approach. They saw life as chronic. When you were born, it was as if you were entering a boat that was going out on the water to eventually sink (die). Consequently, these practitioners were more interested *not* so much in dealing with life's problems as if they all could be solved as they were in greeting each day in ways in which all of life, including—maybe *especially*—pain and suffering were faced mindfully and thus beneficially. This must also be the case with professionals and nonprofessionals in the helping and healing professions seeking to help those who have experienced trauma or great stress.

Once, a young Catholic priest from New Zealand learned this lesson during his first year out of the seminary. He was asked by one of the authors of this *Primer* a question he asks of all clinical psychologists, counselors, social workers, psychiatrists, nurses, chaplains, physicians, and persons in full-time ministry after they have been out of training for a while; namely, "Since completion of your courses and fieldwork, is there a certain interaction that stands out for you as a memorable learning experience?" In response, the priest shared what he felt was his most teachable moment in the year since his ordination:

> I received a message that I was needed at the hospital, but the young person who took the message failed to also leave the name of the individual requesting my visit. Since the hospital was a small one I decided to take a chance and visit there anyway to see if I could find out who called for me. When I entered the entryway to the hospital I could see a distressed couple in the corner: He was crying and she looked desolate.
>
> I took a chance, walked over, introduced myself, and asked if they had called for a priest to visit. They responded affirmatively and told me that it was they who had called. They then explained that they had just given birth to twins and one was born alive but the other was born dead. We then went down into the morgue and stood around the little figure covered by a shroud, and we prayed and we cried.
>
> Then, almost like a resurrection experience, we went up the stairs to the neonatal intensive care unit to visit the other child. When we entered the unit, it was a totally different experience. Unlike the morgue, there was real life there. The walls were brightly painted, mobiles hung from the ceiling, there was a lot of chatter and energy. We then stood around the incubator and prayed and cried again—but this time, they were tears of joy.
>
> Then after a pause, the priest added,
>
> The lesson for me in this poignant encounter was: I don't think I would have been able to cry those tears of joy if I

hadn't first cried those tears of sadness. For good things to be experienced, I must be willing to face directly those which don't feel good at all.

In this brief volume, the goal has been to mine the empirical and theoretical material on posttraumatic growth in order to provide insight and practical guidance to help clients encounter negative events—in particular, traumatic ones—in the most beneficial manner possible. The goal was not to force good things to happen to traumatized people but to be open to new possibilities to make the most of that period when the crisis is past. There is a psychological light within and at the end of the tunnel, as well as the paradoxical opportunity for clients to truly benefit in ways that would not have been possible if the tragedy or significant sad event had not happened in the first place.

When posttraumatic growth occurs, we begin to appreciate that:

It is not the amount of darkness in the world that matters. It is not even the amount of darkness in ourselves that matters. In the end, it is how we stand in that darkness that is of essence. (Wicks, 2010, p. 164)

There is a Zen proverb that we think other world spiritualities would support, which gently suggests, "If you relax and make yourself comfortable, you can journey anywhere." In the therapeutic setting for posttraumatic growth to occur and be reinforced, this is exactly what we as clinicians seek to do: But what about *us* as the guides and helpers in this process? In the pilgrimage through trauma and personal darkness with others, a client's life can be truly defined within those unwanted times—and so can ours.

Although traumatic stress is undesirable, it can take *both* clients and clinicians to places in themselves and their lives in ways never encountered before *if* they have the wherewithal to see and embrace the promise such experiences *might* offer. (Once again, such growth cannot and should not be forced by or *within* the clients or, for that matter, by the clinicians themselves as well.)

In psychological darkness caused by trauma and serious stress, humility potentially comes into play as people see how little control they have over life and how much is overlooked or never unwrapped in their lives. Gratefulness for that can now be embraced. This recognition is crucial, because when humility is added to that which comes during a dark period in life, acknowledge it can then become new wisdom. When you add this wisdom to compassion, it has an opportunity to become selfless love (Wicks, 2012). As clinicians, we must at least consider this hypothesis concerning humility when reviewing our caseloads and our own life.

When there is a true acceptance by persons of the reality and tragedy of a traumatic loss (and in some cases a recognition that they would still trade *all* of their posttraumatic growth if they could miraculously undo the cause of the trauma—for example, death of a child), evidencing previously unexpressed mindfulness, perspective, gratitude, happiness, freedom, creativity, courage, forgiveness, acceptance, patience, openness, and *hope* become possible.

Renowned United Kingdom and American publisher Harold Evans (2009), in his memoir *My Paper Chase*, told a story of his daughter when she was young in which he noted the following interaction between the two of them:

> Around the time of 9/11, Isabel, then eleven, was asked at school whether she was British or American. She said she was "Amerikish." Some months after 9/11 her homework for a class in Greek mythology was to make a Pandora's box. We asked her what she'd put in it. She showed us an empty plate for hunger, a Tylenol bottle for disease, a cracked mirror for vanity, and a chocolate for greed. There was also a tiny colored drawing she had made of the Stars and Stripes.

"And that?" we asked.

"Hope," she said.

I often think of that today. (p. 539)

Once again, a key question this primer and hopeful book has then been focusing on is: Are we as clinicians in tune to both the potential appearances and ways of enhancing posttraumatic growth? And are we aware of both the techniques and quality of presence we as clinicians must offer so our clients can make the most of such possibilities if they present themselves (given the limitations of personality and other factors), including the ones that honor the shifts from:

- Fear to courage and patience
- Assuming permanence in life to appreciating the reality of impermanence
- The necessity of posttraumatic self-centeredness to lead to eventual acceptance and a sense of deeper compassion toward them

Naturally, these are but three movements in posttraumatic growth presented in this book. However, as we close our discussion, they provide us with a way of encouraging our thinking about them as well as the other ones you will discover in your own clinical work and the other books recommended throughout this primer.

From Fear to Courage and Patience

Author Bell Hooks (2000) had a longtime relationship dissolve. Of the reactions she reported, the one that seemed so powerful and poignant was *fear*. She wrote in her book, *All About Love*:

My grief was a heavy, despairing sadness caused by parting from a companion of many years but, more important, it was a despair rooted in the fear that love did not exist, could not be found. And even if it were lurking somewhere, I might never know it in my lifetime. It had become hard for me to continue to believe in love's promise when everywhere I turned the enchantment of power or the terror of fear overshadowed the will to love. (p. xvi)

If we multiply this fear, it is akin to that endured in clients experiencing posttraumatic stress. When we as clinicians encounter it, we may even feel it deep within ourselves, and it may have a long psychological shelf life for us. In his classic work, *On Being a Therapist*, Kottler (1989) notes:

Never mind that we catch our clients' colds and flus, what about their pessimism, negativity. . . . Words creep back to haunt us. Those silent screams remain deafening. (p. 8)

Recognizing the seeds of acute secondary stress (also known as vicarious PTSD) with a sense of pacing, perseverance, and courage on our part helps us to continue to work in an optimum way. Not only does it help us survive, but like in the case of our clients who experience posttraumatic growth, it also helps us grow and deepen in ways we might never have expected.

We can see as clinicians that the road to recovery and possible new growth can be a very long one. Patience is the sibling of courage in the journey toward posttraumatic growth, so if we are to be mindful co-journeyers, we need to recognize this with respect to ourselves as well as others supporting the client. We can get a key as to this approach from contemplative and author of *Seven Story Mountain*, Thomas Merton.

He had encountered an elderly religious brother in his abbey who seemed to be on the edge of despair and he asked him what was the matter. In response the brother said that he felt he was losing his spiritual energy, his perspective, maybe even his faith. To this, Merton smiled, put his hand gently on the man's shoulder and said, "Brother, courage comes and goes. Hold on for the next supply." (Mott, 1984, p. 263)

One of the main elements for the clinician in working with clients who experience posttraumatic stress disorder and those who have experienced severe stress, personal loss, or hurt, is *patience*. The client may be impatient, the family and circle of friends often push the person to move on, and, possibly surprisingly, the clinicians may also fall victim to their desire for the client to improve or to be somehow fixed. Patience, pacing, and an eye to possible new insights that clients might achieve can make all the difference.

For instance, once there was a client who had been sexually abused as a child and had all but repressed this reality. Later on in life she started to become aware of it and became depressed. During the therapy, she reported to the counselor that each morning she would get up and go down to have breakfast and a morning chat with those she lived with, but she dismissed the importance of it by saying, "I only did this because I didn't want them to know I was feeling so badly." To which the therapist responded, "You may feel that, but the other reality is that you are able to get out of bed and interact despite how you feel. Others are not able to do this; *you* are. Given this, please make a list of any positive actions—no matter how you view the real reasons you have for doing them—that you take like this, so we can see them more clearly for what they are: acts of courage."

In the clinician responding this way the client was able to see how she was casting her actions in a totally dismissive fashion when the reality was otherwise. If the clinician is able to be patient and focus—and in turn help the client become more aware—of the progress that is present amidst the gray, depressive outlook that is present after trauma, then such patient attention to greater clarity could open the door to new insights, a decrease in fear, and the recognition that in the client's dealing with this trauma directly it shows evidence of the courage the client has exhibited but may not even be aware of or is currently playing down. Yet, for this to happen, it helps if clinicians have the same patience for themselves and their growth—whether they have experienced a terrible tragedy in their lives or not. Once again, in our own life as well as our clinical practice, we must remember as well: Courage comes and goes. Hold on for the next supply.

From Assuming Permanence in Life to Accepting the Reality of Impermanence

No one likes personal darkness. Nor should he or she. Yet, as we have noted, at times there is just no way around it. Instead, the option lies for us as therapists in *how* we respond to trauma, severe loss, great crises, and deep sadness to the unfolding of our clients' past and new narratives as well as our own.

As we realize, darkness crushes and embitters some people. Others may seek to ignore the impact of the trauma and hope it will just eventually go away, which it rarely does. Or, they—often with the help of a healthy, informed therapeutic presence in their life—may persistently (but at times not patiently) face the trauma and severe stress clearly and compassionately with the help of the therapist, so it can soften and teach them new lessons in living.

The lessons learned may not return the traumatized to where they were before the darkness occurred: Nothing usually can do that. Yet, as we have noted previously in this book, the literature that is building shows that with time, reflection, support, hard work, and openness, some people may in fact be led to places within themselves and in their life that they would have never reached otherwise. There is no magic in this. As a matter of fact, it begins to a great extent with the acceptance of an important reality: An *irreversible change* has occurred in their lives.

Someone dear has been killed or died, abuse or rape has taken place, a childhood has been lost, a reputation has been forever ruined, war atrocities have been seen and maybe participated in. Again, a permanent change to this person or community has occurred. Nothing can alter that. To the clinician who is interested in posttraumatic growth, the obvious question of value that is in the fore—with no preordained answer or time frame because each person and situation is unique—is that after the trauma or serious stress has occurred: *Now what?*

For those clinicians, possibly through their own mindfulness meditation practice that includes an openness to the fragility of life and a sense of the reality of impermanence as well as a knowledge of posttraumatic growth,[1] there is a ready preparation to sit with persons dealing with confronting the reality of having encountered an irreversible, unwanted change in their lives. Clinicians who are aware of the recognition that birth always ends in death, gathering with releasing, and meeting with leaving may then be freer—have greater space within—to be more compassionate and focus on their clients rather than on themselves, because their own existential fear of death and unwanted change has remained ignored, denied, or unprocessed.

In clinical supervision, we may have heard or as supervisors ourselves made the recommendation, "Teach through modeling; if necessary, use words." Nowhere is this more the case than in the appreciation of the reality of impermanence in all of our lives, and on the impact of how one lives, if the lesson is constantly before us.

---

[1] See books listed at the end of this epilogue for further recommended reading on informal and formal mindfulness (meditation) that may be of particular interest to clinicians.

From Self-Centeredness to Acceptance and Compassion

Initially, when a crisis or trauma occurs, as well as fear and exposure to the stark reality of impermanence, people also tend to pull in on themselves. In the beginning that's natural and good. People who have experienced trauma can't take too much outside stimuli. They need room to acknowledge, grieve, adjust, let go—*survive*. This is no less the case with clinicians, because they are being bombarded with trauma in their clinical practice as well as, on occasion, at home. If clinicians believe that compassion is good, then certainly they must include *themselves* as well. However, how they undertake this can be crucial during both the session and within the ongoing process of treatment.

There is an old psychodynamic adage that clinicians cannot take their clients any further in treatment than they have gone themselves. Whether this is accurate or not is arguable, but it is probably true that for clinicians to be sensitive to the delicate process of posttraumatic growth in others, they must, at the very least, have the space within themselves to increase the odds that progress is both possible and achievable. Defensiveness and a fractious ego hold both the therapy and the therapist back, especially during the therapy undertaken with clients who have experienced intense stress, trauma, and loss.

At some point trauma survivors must look outside of themselves if they are to continue progress. Otherwise, the ironic result in focusing solely on the loss, trauma, crisis, or perpetrator will be for that person to chain themselves unconsciously to the pain. At some point, for posttraumatic growth to become possible and blossom, there must be a letting go or, more appropriately, a living with the trauma in a new way. Some of the monks who were tortured by their jailors in Chinese prisons recognized this to an incredible degree. One even said to the Dalai Lama after his escape that he was "afraid that one day he might lose his sympathy for his Chinese captors" (Iyer, 2008, p. 48). Quite amazing.

However, for compassion not based on duty or guilt to be rich for both trauma victims and the clinicians who treat them, healthy self-centeredness (appropriate self-care/understanding/love) is necessary. Once this takes root and there are signs that new growth is present (i.e., the therapy is not as focused on what happened in the past but is more now/future-focused, and the person seems more empowered than is self-defining as a victim), then compassionate action is part of the movement toward integrating posttraumatic growth.

It may begin, for instance, with a rape or abuse victim safely expressing anger at others who have been traumatized. However, at a certain juncture later in the treatment when a fuller acceptance of what has happened leads to new personal growth and depth, then a defensive-free interest in others starts to evidence itself. Persons or survivor groups that stay focused on themselves forever and don't look out of themselves or the groups are, in the experience of the authors, a clinical indication that posttraumatic growth might not take place. Returning to the example of the compassionate Tibetan monks who were tortured, we see such an example. One older monk asks another if he feels compassion now toward his former captors. The other responds vehemently, "Never!" to which the more senior monk softly responds, "Well, they still have you in prison then, don't they?"

The Mindful Clinician

In this brief epilogue we have moved beyond the empirical literature to take a breath and reflect on what it is like to be a mindful clinician working with those clients experiencing the potential of posttraumatic growth. In doing this, we not only touched on some of the more important points made in this book but also emphasized what we believe to be one of the more important catalysts to posttraumatic growth: the knowledgeable, mindful presence of the clinician.

When the clinician is mindful (in the now and open), then the stage is set for possible growth—not only in the client but in the clinician as well. A wise clinician (and therefore one who is well aware of his or her personal limitations—has a degree of true humility) appreciates the need to:

- Honor life's fragility.
- Be mindful so that less in life is missed or judged to be unworthy of examining and providing new learning.
- Let go of the whys at some point so experience of the now—and not just cognitively—becomes a possible outcome.
- Have their own good self-care regimen and healing rituals in life so compassion toward those who are poised for posttraumatic growth is not simply a psychological duty but a natural expression of the full self.
- Recognize that we as clinicians surprisingly make war with ourselves at times because of a desire to control the uncontrollable both in ourselves and our clinical outcomes in unrealistic ways.
- Appreciate the value of simplicity in how we both view and live life as an intentional approach to periods of silence and solitude for reflection and mindfulness.
- Have a willingness to face our own *koans* (life puzzles) that have no easy answers to them but require choices that will affect our lives.

With such fruits of personal and clinical maturity as these and others, which come from a sense of mindfulness and personal awareness, we can even more completely then take to heart what researchers have provided for us with respect to enhancing the process of posttraumatic growth when it appears. We can then see more clearly so we can in turn guide our clients who have experienced trauma and serious stress to appreciate the following, if and when they might be open to these clinical and life realities:

- Our current basic set of assumptions will not always work; life changes and so must our outlook.
- Loss of control, meaning, and predictability will always occur at times; how we perceive this and respond accordingly is the key to personal growth and depth.
- No one wants trauma, serious stress, and sadness, but they can teach us in the long run new lifelong lessons—*if* we are able to let them.
- Perception and priorities that change in response to experiencing trauma can alter one's philosophy of life in previously unforeseen, rewarding ways (i.e., a richer narrative about one's own personal life).
- Openness to and awareness of the process of growth by and in clients with no preconceived expectations and need for them to undergo the experience is essential for posttraumatic growth to occur in a timely fashion. (Note: One of the best ways for clinicians to prepare for this is for them to use the same approach to growth in themselves in their own therapy, supervision, self-awareness review, and during periods of alonetime in silence, solitude, and mindful meditation.)
- Welcome the appearance of new positive meaning-making post trauma as something filled with potential rather than simply a form of resistance or denial. (This is so when there is also a full recognition of the adverse nature of the event present.)
- Appreciate the sometimes underrated personality aspects of curiosity and openness that play a significant role in determining whether posttraumatic growth will be possible.

- Understand the significant impact of the *absence* of negative social support in the development of posttraumatic growth.
- Remember to consider the broader cultural context that may encourage or discourage growth.
- Explore the role of openness to forgiveness and compassion (as distinct from reconciliation or forgetting) when the timing is right.
- Appreciate that psychological researchers have offered studies on growth after trauma, but that there is much nonempirical wisdom literature that predates this (such as works by Frankl and Yalom, as well as on mindfulness and spiritual approaches to suffering that are both theistic and atheistic such as Buddhism) that in the spirit of learning widely and deeply about posttraumatic growth would benefit the clinician both personally and professionally to access it.
- Appreciate that posttraumatic growth is *not* based simply on a positive reframing of a negative event but a *simultaneous* honoring of it while being open to possibly unforeseeable growth that might not have occurred if the significant stress or traumatic event had not happened.
- Discern between the size of the distress caused for the client and the severity of the trauma itself since the *former* is actually of greater import in terms of impact.
- Flow with client narratives that move from avoidance to approachment via the use of myths as bridges to new philosophical/psychological/spiritual solid ground for them.
- Be sensitive to meaning-making cycles where discrepancies between global and situational belief systems occur.
- Discern the differences between client ruminations that are constructive and deliberate and ones that are intrusive, as well as ones that are positive or negative, and how they can have an important impact on posttraumatic growth.

- Fathom the importance of perception, especially in post-traumatic beliefs about having lost one's way in life. (Daniel Boone was once reported to retort to a question as to whether given his tracking skills that he had ever gotten lost: "No. But I was bewildered once for three days.")
- Acknowledge the subtle, yet crucial, roles that patience and pacing play in working with clients on the journey toward posttraumatic growth (as well as on our own life journey as well).
- Explore the role of relationships before, during, and after the experience of trauma or significant stress; as was previously noted, this is especially so with respect to uncovering the *absence* of negative support.
- Discuss the place that faith, religious community, image of god, spiritual strength, and other related religious themes have if and when they arise in the therapy; from a multicultural vantage point, religious and spiritual aspects are essential to note and are sometimes overlooked aspects of treatment that can adversely impact the flow of posttraumatic growth if they are not recognized and worked with as a deterrent or enhancement to the growth process.

Some Final Comments

Through reflection on the material provided at the end of each chapter, further reading on posttraumatic growth, and personal therapeutic encounters, the clinician will see many more thematic shifts than the ones mentioned in both this chapter and the book as a whole.

Each client, as a result of personality, type of trauma, history, support, and faith experience, among other things, will respond in different ways. That is to be expected. However, the knowledge and readiness about posttraumatic growth that the clinician possesses can make all the difference in capitalizing on these movements by the client if and when they occur.

Are the seeds for posttraumatic growth nurtured, ignored, prematurely planted, and even inadvertently crushed by the counselor, or are they helped to grow? That is the essential question that was confronted here. Given this, the goal to become more mindful, sensitive, and better equipped to begin looking for more suitable responses to the increasing number of clients going through a posttrauma experience and poised for new growth *because* of what they have experienced, is truly a worthy one. Consequently, any knowledge of the process of posttraumatic growth gained in this book and through further reading, Continuing Education Units (CEUs), and supervised experience should prove very rewarding to both the clinician's sense of competence with this population and result in more informed guidance for those who would go deeper and become more sensitive because of what they have experienced. When this occurs, it is a very moving experience for all.

Trauma may leave gifts in its wake. Surprisingly, clients—and clinicians at times—may fail to open them. One possible reason is quite simply they don't know the gifts are there. They are invisible because the trauma victim and counselor neither expect nor look for them. In this book they were highlighted to reduce the chances that this will happen. Yet, it can't be emphasized enough, that even when clinicians are fully aware, there is still no guarantee that posttraumatic growth will occur. As is obvious by now, forcing growth is clinically immature and not in line with either appreciating that the client may never grow but with counseling hopefully return to a degree of functioning that parallels to some extent the premorbid state. Posttraumatic growth education is about *possibility*: recognizing it and taking advantage of it while not forcing it. Hopefully, this book has helped in beginning to provide guidance for you in this very subtle and important process.

Selected References

Joseph, S. (2011). *What doesn't kill us: The new psychology of posttraumatic growth.* New York, NY: Basic Books.
This is one of the most recent books available on posttraumatic growth. Written for nonprofessionals by one of the leading experts in the field, it is ideal to use as part of a bibliotherapy regimen with clients at an advanced point in the treatment as a way of helping them understand the process they have gone through as well as prepare them for what is ahead. This is also an excellent next book to read after completing this *Primer on Posttraumatic Growth: An Introduction and Guide.*

Recommended Readings on Mindfulness of Special Relevance for Clinicians

Batchelor, S. (1997). *Buddhism without beliefs.* New York, NY: Riverhead.

Beck, C. (1989). *Everyday Zen: Love and work.* San Francisco, CA: Harper San Francisco.

Brach, T. (2003). *Radical acceptance: Embracing your life with the heart of a Buddha.* New York, NY: Bantam Dell.

Brantley, J. (2003). *Calming your anxious mind.* Oakland, CA: New Harbinger.

Brazier, D. (1995). *Zen therapy: Transcending the sorrows of the human mind.* New York, NY: Wiley.

Chodron, P. (2001). *The wisdom of no escape and the path of loving-kindness.* Boston, MA: Shambhala.

Dalai Lama & Cutler, H. (1998). *The art of happiness: A handbook for living.* New York, NY: Riverhead.

Epstein, M. (1995). *Thoughts without a thinker: Psychotherapy from a Buddhist perspective.* New York, NY: Basic Books.

Germer, C., Siegel, R., & Fulton, P. (Eds.). (2005). *Mindfulness and psychotherapy.* New York, NY: Guilford Press.

Goldman, D. (2003). *Destructive emotions: How can we overcome them?* New York, NY: Bantam Dell.

Goldstein, J. (1993). *Insight meditation: The practice of freedom.* Boston, MA: Shambhala.

Goldstein, J., & Kornfield, J. (1987). *Seeking the heart of wisdom.* Boston, MA: Shambhala.

Gunaratana, B. (2002). *Mindfulness in plain English.* Somerville, MA: Wisdom.

Hanh, T. N. (1975/1987). *The miracle of mindfulness.* Boston: Beacon Press.

Hayes, S., Follette, V., & Linehan, M. (Eds.). (2004). *Mindfulness and acceptance: Expanding the cognitive-behavioral tradition.* New York, NY: Guilford Press.

Kabat-Zinn, J. (1990). *Full catastrophe living.* New York, NY: Delacorte Press.

Kabat-Zinn, J. (1994). *Wherever you go, there you are: Mindfulness meditation in everyday life.* New York, NY: Hyperion.

Kabat-Zinn, J. (2005). *Coming to our senses: Healing ourselves and the world through mindfulness.* New York, NY: Hyperion.

Kabat-Zinn, J. (2005). *Guided mindfulness meditation. Series 1-3* [Compact disc]. P. O. Box 547, Lexington, MA. Stress Reduction CDs and Tapes.

Kabat-Zinn, M., & Kabat-Zinn, J. (1998). *Everyday blessings: The inner work of mindful parenting.* New York, NY: Hyperion.

Kornfield, J. (1993). *A path with heart: A guide through the perils and promises of spiritual life.* New York, NY: Bantam.

Kornfield, J. (2000). *After the ecstasy, the laundry: How the heart grows wise on the spiritual path.* New York, NY: Bantam.

Langer, E. (1989). *Mindfulness.* Cambridge, MA: Da Capo Press.

Linehan, M. (2005). *This one moment: Skills for everyday mindfulness.* Seattle, WA: Behavioral Tech.

Salzberg, S. (1995). *Loving kindness: The revolutionary art of happiness.* Boston, MA: Shambhala.

Stern, D. (2004). *The present moment in psychotherapy and everyday life.* New York, NY: W. W. Norton.

Suzuki, S. (1973). *Zen mind, beginner's mind.* New York, NY: John Weatherhill.

Weiss, A. (2004). *Beginning mindfulness: Learning the way of awareness.* Novato, CA: New World Library.

Wicks, R. (2003). *Riding the dragon.* Notre Dame, IL: Soren Books.

Wicks, R. (2008). *The resilient clinician.* New York, NY: Oxford University Press.

References

Abraido-Lanza, A. F., Guier, C., & Colon, R. M. (1998). Psychological thriving among Latinas with chronic illness. *Journal of Social Issues, 54,* 405–424.

Ai, A. L., Cascio, T., Santangelo, L. K., & Evans-Campball, T. (2005). Hope, meaning and growth following the September 11, 2001 terrorist attacks. *Journal of Interpersonal Violence, 20,* 523–548.

Albert, S. (1977). Temporal comparison theory. *Psychological Review, 84,* 485–503.

Allport, G. W., & Ross, J. M. (1967). Personal religioius orientation and prejudice. *Journal of Personality and Social Psychology, 5,* 432–443.

American Psychiatric Association. (1980). *Diagnostic and statistical manual of mental disorders* (3rd ed.; DSM-III). Washington, DC: Author.

American Psychiatric Association. (2000). *Diagnostic and statistical manual of mental disorders* (4th ed., text rev.; DSM-IV-TR). Washington, DC: Author.

Ano, A. G., & Vasconcelles, E. B. (2005). Religious coping and psychological adjustment to stress: A meta-analysis. *Journal of Clinical Psychology, 61,* 461–480.

Anonymous. (2007). The impact that changed my life. *Professional Psychology: Research and Practice, 38,* 561–570.

Antoni, M. H., Lehman, J. M., Kilbourn, K. M., Boyers, A. E., Culver, J. L., Alferi, S. M., . . . Carver, C. S. (2001). Cognitive-behavioral stress management intervention decreases the prevalence of depression and enhances benefit finding among women under treatment for early-stage breast cancer. *Health Psychology, 20,* 20–32.

Aquinas, T. (1945). *Summa contra gentiles.* A. C. Pegis (Trans.). New York, NY: Random House.

Aspinwall, L. G., Richter, L., & Hoffman, R. R. (2001). Understanding how optimism "works": An examination of optimists' adaptive moderation of belief and behavior. In E. C. Chang (Ed.), *Optimism and pessimism: Theory, research, and practice* (pp. 217–238). Washington, DC: American Psychological Association.

Bade, M. K., & Cook, S. W. (2008). Functions of Christian prayer in the coping process. *Journal for the Scientific Study of Religion, 47,* 123–133.

Bandura, A. (1995). *Self-efficacy in changing societies.* Cambridge, UK: Cambridge University Press.

Batson, C. D., Schoenrade, P., & Ventis, W. L. (1993). *Religion and the individual: A social-psychological perspective.* New York, NY: Oxford University Press.

Baumeister, R. F. (1991). *Meanings in life.* New York, NY: Guilford Press.

Baumeister, R. F., & Leary, M. R. (1995). The need to belong: Desire for interpersonal attachments as a fundamental human motivation. *Psychological Bulletin, 117,* 497–529.

Baumeister, R. F., & Vohs, K. D. (2002). The pursuit of meaningfulness in life. In C. Snyder & S. Lopez (Eds.), *The handbook of positive psychology* (pp. 608–628). New York, NY: Oxford University Press.

Bemporad, J. (2005). Suffering. In L. Jones, M. Eliade, & C. J. Adams (Eds.), *Encyclopedia of religion* (pp. 8804–8809). Detroit, MI: Macmillan.

Bowlby, J. (1988). *A secure base: Parent-child attachment and healthy human development.* New York, NY: Basic Books.

Boy, A. V., & Pine, G. J. (1999). *A person-centered foundation for counseling and psychotherapy.* Springfield, IL: Charles C. Thomas.

Boyraz, G., & Efstathiou, N. (2011). Self-focused attention, meaning, and posttraumatic growth: Mediating role of positive and negative affect for bereaved women. *Journal of Loss and Trauma, 16*, 13–32.

Brazier, D. (1995). *Zen therapy: Transcending the sorrows of the human mind.* New York, NY: Wiley.

Brewin, C. R. (2003). *Posttraumatic stress disorder: Malady or myth?* New Haven, CT: Yale University Press.

Brim, O. G., & Featherman, D. L. (1998). *Surveying midlife development in the United States.* Unpublished manuscript.

Cadell, S., Regehr, C., & Hemsworth, D. (2003). Factors contributing to posttraumatic growth: A proposed structural equation model. *American Journal of Orthopsychiatry, 73*, 279–287.

Cadell, S., & Sullivan, R. (2006). Posttraumatic growth and HIV bereavement: Where does it start and when does it end? *Traumatology, 12*, 45–59.

Calhoun, L. G., Cann, A. G., Tedeschi, R. G., & McMillan, J. (2000). A correlational test of the relationship between posttraumatic growth, religion, and cognitive processing. *Journal of Traumatic Stress, 13*, 521–527.

Calhoun, L. G., Cann, A. G., & Tedeschi, R. G. (2010). The posttraumatic growth model: Sociocultural considerations. In T. Weiss & R. Berger (Eds.), *Posttraumatic growth and culturally competent practice: Lessons learned from around the globe.* Hoboken, NJ: Wiley.

Calhoun, L. G., & Tedeschi, R. G. (1998). Beyond recovery from trauma: Implications for clinical practice and research. *Journal of Social Issues, 54*, 357–371.

Calhoun, L. G., & Tedeschi, R. G. (1999). *Facilitating posttraumatic growth: A clinician's guide.* Mahwah, NJ: Erlbaum.

Calhoun, L. G., & Tedeschi, R. G. (2006). The foundations of post-traumatic growth: An expanded framework. In L. G. Calhoun & R. G. Tedeschi (Eds.), *Handbook of posttraumatic growth: Research and practice* (pp. 1–23). Mahwah, NJ: Erlbaum.

Camus, A. (1968). *Summer.* London, UK: Penguin.

Cann, A., Calhoun, L. G., Tedeschi, R. G., Taku, K., Vishnevsky, T., Triplett, K. N., & Danhauer, S. C. (2010). A short form of the posttraumatic growth inventory. *Anxiety, Stress, & Coping, 23,* 127–137.

Caplan, G. (1961). *An approach to community mental health.* New York, NY: Grune and Stratton.

Caplan, G. (1964). *Principles of preventive psychiatry.* New York, NY: Basic Books.

Carpenter, J. S., Brockopp, D. Y., & Andrykowski, M. A. (1999). Self-transformation as a factor in the self-esteem and well-being of breast cancer survivors. *Journal of Advanced Nursing, 29,* 1402–1411.

Carver, C. S., & Antoni, M. H. (2004). Finding benefit in breast cancer during the year after diagnosis predicts better adjustment 5 to 8 years after diagnosis. *Health Psychology, 23,* 595–598.

Cataldo, L. M. (2008). Multiple selves, multiple Gods? Functional polytheism and the postmodern patient. *Pastoral Psychology, 57,* 45–58

Cheng, C., Wong, W., & Tsang, K. (2006). Perception of benefits and costs during SARS outbreak: An 18-month prospective study. *Journal of Consulting and Clinical Psychology, 74,* 870–879.

Cohen, S. (2004). Social relationships and health. *American Psychologist, 59,* 676–684.

Cohen, L. H., Hettler, T. R., & Pane, N. (1998). Assessment of posttraumatic growth. In R. G. Tedeschi, C. L. Park, &

L. G. Calhoun, (Eds.), *Posttraumatic growth: Positive changes in the aftermath of crisis* (pp. 22–42). Mahwah, NJ: Erlbaum.

Cordova, M. J., Cunningham, L. C., Carlson, C. R., & Andrykowski, M. A. (2001). Posttraumatic growth following breast cancer: A controlled comparison study. *Health Psychology, 20*, 176–185.

Costa, P. T., & McCrae, R. R. (1992). *NEO-PI-R professional manual.* Lutz, FL: Psychological Assessment Resources.

Crews, C. F. (1986). *Ultimate questions: A theological primer.* Mahwah, NJ: Paulist Press.

Danner, D. D., Snowdon, D. A., & Friesen, W. V. (2001). Positive emotions in early life and longevity: Findings from the nun study. *Journal of Personality and Social Psychology, 2*, 300–319.

Davidson, R. J., Kabat-Zinn, J., Schumacher, J., Rosenkranz, M., Muller, D., Santorelli, S. F., . . . Sheridan, J. F. (2003). Alterations in brain and immune function produced by mindfulness meditation. *Psychosomatic Medicine, 65*, 564–570.

Davis, C. G., Nolen-Hoeksema, S., & Larson, J. (1998). Making sense of loss and growing from the experience: Two construals of meaning. *Journal of Personality and Social Psychology, 75*, 561–574.

Davis, C., Wortman, C., Lehman, D., & Silver, R. (2000). Searching for meaning in loss: Are clinical assumptions correct? *Death Studies, 24*, 497–540.

de Saint-Exupery, A. (1932). *Night flight.* Orlando, FL: Harcourt Brace.

Debats, D. L. (1999). Sources of meaning: An investigation of significant commitments in life. *Journal of Humanistic Psychology, 39*, 30–57.

DeNeve, K. M., & Cooper, H. (1998). The happy personality: A meta-analysis of 137 personality traits and subjective well-being. *Psychological Bulletin, 124*, 197–229.

Diener, E. (1984). Subjective well-being. *Psychological Bulletin, 95,* 542–575.

Digman, J. M. (1996). A curious history of the Five-Factor Model. In J. S. Wiggins (Ed.), *The Five-Factor Model of personality: Theoretical perspectives* (pp. 1–20). New York, NY: Guilford Press.

Engelkemeyer, S. M., & Marwit, S. J. (2008). Posttraumatic growth in bereaved parents. *Journal of Traumatic Stress, 21,* 344–346.

Enright, R. D., & Coyle, C. T. (1998). Researching the process model of forgiveness within psychological interventions. In E. L. Worthington (Ed.), *Dimensions of forgiveness: Psychological research and theological perspectives* (pp. 139–161). Philadelphia, PA: Templeton Foundation Press.

Evans, H. (2009). *My paper chase: True stories of vanished times.* New York, NY: Little, Brown.

Falsetti, S. A., Resick, P. A., & Davis, J. L. (2003). Changes in religious beliefs following trauma. *Journal of Traumatic Stress, 16,* 391–398.

Feder, A., Southwick, S. M., Goetz, R. R., Wang, Y., Alonso, A., Smith, B. W., . . . Vythilingam, M. (2008). Posttraumatic growth in former Vietnam prisoners of war. *Psychiatry, 71,* 359–370.

Festinger, L. (1954). A theory of social comparison process. *Human Relations, 7,* 117–140.

Fincham, F. D., & Kashdan, T. B. (2004). Facilitating forgiveness. In P. A. Linley & S. Joseph (Eds.), *Positive psychology in practice* (pp. 617–637). Hoboken, NJ: Wiley.

Fischer, P. C. (2006). The link between posttraumatic growth and forgiveness: An intuitive truth. In L. G. Calhoun & R. G. Tedeschi (Eds.), *Handbook of posttraumatic growth: Research and practice (pp. 311–333).* Mahwah, NJ: Erlbaum.

Folkman, S. (2008). The case for positive emotions in the stress process. *Anxiety, Stress, & Coping, 21,* 3–14.

Fontana, A., & Rosenheck, R. (2004). Trauma, change in strength of religious faith, and mental health service use among veterans treated for PTSD. *Journal of Nervous and Mental Disease, 192,* 579–584.

Frankl, V. (1963). *Man's search for meaning.* New York, NY: Pocket Books.

Frankl, V. (1969). *The will to meaning: Foundations and applications of logotherapy.* New York, NY: Penguin.

Frazier, P., Conlon, A., & Glaser, T. (2001). Positive and negative life changes following sexual assault. *Journal of Consulting and Clinical Psychology, 69,* 1048–1055.

Frazier, P., & Kaler, P. (2006). Assessing the validity of self-reported stress-related growth. *Journal of Consulting and Clinical Psychology, 74,* 859–869.

Frazier, P., Tennen, H., Gavian, M., Park, C., Tomich, P., & Tashiro, T. (2009). Does self-reported post-traumatic growth reflect genuine positive change? *Psychological Science, 20,* 912–919.

Fredrickson, B. L. (1998). What good are positive emotions? *Review of General Psychology, 2,* 300–319.

Fredrickson, B. L. (2000). Cultivating positive emotions to optimize health and well-being. *Prevention and Treatment, 3.* Available at http://journals.apa.org/prevention/volume3/toc-mar07-00.html.

Fredrickson, B. L. (2001). The role of positive emotions in positive psychology. *American Psychologist, 56,* 218–226.

Fredrickson, B. L., Cohn, M. A., Coffey, K. A., Pek, J., & Finkel, S. M. (2008). Open hearts build lives: Positive emotions, induced through loving-kindness meditation, build consequential personal resources. *Journal of Personality and Social Psychology, 95,* 1045–1062.

Fredrickson, B. L., & Joiner, T. (2002). Positive emotions trigger upward spirals toward emotional well-being. *Psychological Science, 13,* 172–175.

Fredrickson, B. L., & Losada, M. (2005). Positive affect and the complex dynamics of human flourishing. *American Psychologist, 60,* 678–686.

Fredrickson, B. L., Mancuso, R. A., Branigan, C., & Tugade, M. (2000). The undoing effect of positive emotions. *Motivation and Emotion, 24,* 237–258.

Fredrickson, B. L., Tugade, M. M., Waugh, C. E., & Larkin, G. R. (2003). What good are positive emotions in crises? A prospective study of resilience and emotions following the terrorist attacks on the United States on September 11th, 2001. *Journal of Personality and Social Psychology , 84,* 365–376.

Fulton, P. (2005). Mindfulness as clinical training. In C. K Germer, R. D. Siegel, & P. R. Fulton, *Mindfulness and psychotherapy* (pp. 55–72). New York, NY: Guilford Press.

Gangstad, B., Norman, P., & Barton, J. (2009). Cognitive processing and posttraumatic growth after stroke. *Rehabilitation Psychology, 54,* 69–75.

Garland, E. L., Fredrickson, B. L, Kring, A. M., Johnson, D., Meyer, P. S., & Penn, D. L. (2010). Upward spirals of positive emotions counter downward spirals of negativity: Insights from broaden-and-build theory and affective neuroscience on treatment of emotion dysfunctions and deficits in psychopathology. *Clinical Psychology Review, 30,* 849–864.

Garnefski, N., Kraaij, V., Schroevers, M., & Somsen, G. (2008). Post-traumatic growth after a myocardial infarction: A matter of personality, psychological health, or cognitive coping? *Journal of Clinical Psychology in Medical Settings, 15,* 270–277.

Grubaugh, A. L., & Resick, P. A. (2007). Posttraumatic growth in treatment-seeking female assault victims. *Psychiatric Quarterly, 78,* 145–155.

Guidano, V. (1995). Self-observation in constructivist psychotherapy. In R. A. Neimeyer & M. J. Mahoney (Eds.), *Constructivism in psychotherapy* (pp. 155–168). Washington, DC: American Psychological Association.

Gunty, A., Frazier, P., Tennen, H., Tomich, P., Tashiro, T., & Park, C. (2011). Moderators of the relation between perceived and actual posttraumatic growth. *Psychological Trauma: Theory, Research, Practice, and Policy, 3,* 61–66.

Hall, M. E. L., & Johnson, E. L. (2001). Theodicy and therapy: Philosophical/theological contributions to the problem of suffering. *Journal of Psychology and Spirituality, 20,* 5–17.

Halpern, H. A. (1973). Crisis theory: A definitional study. *Community Mental Health Journal, 9,* 342–349.

Harms, L., & Talbot, M. (2007). The aftermath of road trauma: Survivors perceptions of trauma and growth. *Health and Social Work, 32,* 129–137.

Harrington, D. (2000). *Why do we suffer? A scriptural approach to the human condition.* Franklin, WI: Sheed & Ward.

Harris, J. I., Erbes, C. R., Engdahl, B. E., Olson, R. H. A., Winskowski, A. M., & McMahill, J. (2008). Christian religious functioning and trauma outcomes. *Journal of Clinical Psychology, 64,* 17–29.

Hauser, R. J. (1994). *Finding God in troubled times.* Chicago, IL: Loyola University Press.

Helgeson, V. S., Reynolds, K. A., & Tomich P. L. (2006). A meta-analytic review of benefit finding and growth. *Journal of Consulting and Clinical Psychology, 74,* 797–816.

Henderson, A. S., & Brown, G. W. (1988). Social support: The hypothesis and the evidence. In S. Henderson & G. D. Burrows (Eds.), *Handbook of Social Psychiatry* (pp. 73–85). Amsterdam, The Netherlands: Elsevier.

Holahan, C., Moos, R., & Schaefer, J. (1996). Coping, stress resistance, and growth. In M. Zeidner & N. S. Endler (Eds.), *The handbook of stress and coping: Theory, research, and applications* (pp. 24–43). New York, NY: Free Press.

Hood, R. W. Jr., Spilka, B., Hunsberger, B., & Gorsuch, R. (1996). *The psychology of religion: An empirical approach* (2nd ed.). New York, NY: Guilford Press.

Hooks, B. (2000). *All about love: New visions.* New York, NY: Morrow.

Iyer, P. (2008). *The open road: The global journey of the fourteenth Dalai Lama.* New York, NY: Knopf.

Janoff-Bulman, R. (1992). *Shattered assumptions: Towards a new psychology of trauma.* New York, NY: Free Press.

Janoff-Bulman, R., & Frantz, C. M. (1997). The impact of trauma on meaning: From a meaningless world to a meaningful life. In M. J. Power & C. R. Brewin (Eds.), *The transformation of meaning in psychological therapies: Integrating theory and practice* (pp. 91–106). New York, NY: Wiley.

Joseph, S. (2004). Client-centered therapy, post-traumatic stress disorders and post-traumatic growth: Theoretical perspectives and practical implications. *Psychology and Psychotherapy: Theory, Research, and Practice, 77,* 101–119.

Joseph, S. (2011). *What doesn't kill us: The new psychology of posttraumatic growth.* New York, NY: Basic Books.

Joseph, S., & Linley, P. A. (2005). Positive adjustment to threatening events: An organismic valuing theory of growth through adversity. *Review of General Psychology, 9,* 262–280.

Joseph, S., & Linley, P. A. (2006). Growth following adversity: Theoretical perspectives and implications for clinical practice. *Clinical Psychology Review, 26,* 1041–1053.

Joseph, S., & Linley, P. (2008). Psychological assessment of growth following adversity: A review. In S. Joseph & P. A. Linley (Eds.), *Trauma, recovery, and growth: Positive psychological perspectives on posttraumatic stress* (pp. 21–36). Hoboken, NJ: Wiley.

Joseph, S., Linley, P. A., Shevlin, M., Goodfellow, B., & Butler, L. (2006). Assessing positive and negative changes in the aftermath of adversity: A short form of the Changes in Outlook Questionnaire. *Journal of Loss and Trauma, 11,* 85–89.

Joseph, S., Williams, R., & Yule, W. (1993). Changes in outlook following disaster: The preliminary development of a measure to assess positive and negative responses. *Journal of Traumatic Stress, 6,* 271–279.

Karen, R. (1998). *Becoming attached: First relationships and how they shape our capacity to love.* New York, NY: Oxford University Press.

Kiecolt-Glaser, J. K., & Glaser, R. (1992). Stress and the immune system: Human studies. *American Psychiatric Press Review of Psychiatry, 11,* 169–180.

King, L. A., Hicks, J. A., Krull, J., & Del Gaiso, A. (2006). Positive affect and the experience of meaning in life. *Journal of Personality and Social Psychology, 90,* 179–196.

Klinger, E. (1998). The search for meaning in evolutionary perspective and its clinical implications. In P. T. P. Wong & P. Fry (Eds.), *The human quest for meaning* (pp. 27–50). Mahwah, NJ: Erlbaum.

Koenig, H. G. (2004). Religion, spirituality, and medicine: Research findings and implications for clinical practice. *Southern Medical Journal, 97,* 1194–1200.

Koenig, H.G. (March, 2010). *Understanding the effects of religious coping and health.* Speech presented at the American Psychological Association Division 36 Psychology of Religion Annual Meeting. Columbia, MD.

Koenig, H. G., Pargament, K. I., & Nielsen, J. (1998). Religious coping and health status in medically ill hospitalized older adults. *Journal of Nervous and Mental Disease, 186,* 513–521.

Kottler, J. (1989). *On being a therapist.* San Francisco, CA: Jossey-Bass.

Lara, M. E., Leader, J., & Klein, D. N. (1997). The association between social support and course of depression: Is it confounded with personality? *Journal of Abnormal Psychology, 106,* 478–482.

Laufer, A., Raz-Hamama, Y., Levine, S., & Solomon, Z. (2009). Post-traumatic growth in adolescence: The role of religiosity, distress, and forgiveness. *Journal of Social and Clinical Psychology, 28*, 862–880.

Lazarus, R. S., & Folkman, S. (1987). Transaction theory and the research on emotion and coping. *European Journal of Personality, 1*, 141–169.

Lechner, S,. & Antoni, M. (2004). Posttraumatic growth and group-based interventions for persons dealing with cancer: What have we learned so far? *Psychological Inquiry, 15*, 35–41.

Lechner, S. C., Stoelb, B. L., & Antoni, M. H. (2008). Group-based therapies for benefit finding in cancer. In S. Joseph & P. A. Linley (Eds.), *Trauma, recovery, and growth: Positive psychological perspectives on posttraumatic stress* (pp. 207–231). Hoboken, NJ: Wiley.

Lepore, S. J., Evans, G. W., & Schneider, M. L. (1991). Dynamic role of social support in the link between chronic stress and psychological distress. *Journal of Personality and Social Psychology, 61*, 899–909.

Lepore, S. J., & Revenson, T. (2006). *Relationships between posttraumatic growth and resilience: Recovery, resistance & reconfiguration.* In L. G. Calhoun & R. G. Tedeschi (Eds.), *Handbook of posttraumatic growth: Research and practice* (pp. 24–46). Mahwah, NJ: Erlbaum.

Levine, E. G., Aviv, C., Yoo, G., Ewing, C., & Au, A. (2009). The benefits of prayer on mood and well being of breast cancer survivors. *Supportive Care in Cancer, 17*, 295–306.

Levine, S. Z., Laufer, A., Hamama-Raz, Y., Stein, E., & Solomon, Z. (2008). Posttraumatic growth in adolescence: Examining its components and relationship with PTSD. *Journal of Traumatic Stress, 21*, 492–496.

Lewis, C. S. (1961). *A grief observed.* San Francisco, CA: Harper Collins.

Liderbach, D. (1992). *Why do we suffer? New ways of understanding.* Mahwah, NJ: Paulist Press.

Linley, P. A., & Joseph, S. (2004). Positive change following trauma and adversity: A review. *Journal of Traumatic Stress, 17*, 11–21.

Lyubomirsky, S. (2007). *The how of happiness: A new approach to getting the life you want.* New York, NY: Penguin.

Maddux, J. E. (2002). The power of believing in you. In C. R. Snyder & S. J. Lopez, *Oxford handbook of positive psychology* (pp. 335–344). New York, NY: Oxford University Press.

Maercker, A. (1998). *Posttraumatische Belastungsstörungen: Psychologie der xtrembelastungsfolgen bei Opfern politischer Gewalt* [Posttraumatic stress disorder: Psychology of extreme distress in victims of political violence]. Lengerich, Germany: Pabst.

Maercker, A., & Zoellner, T. (2004). The Janus face of self-perceived growth: Toward a two-component model of posttraumatic growth. *Psychological Inquiry, 15,* 41–48.

Magnus, K., Diener, E., Fujita, F., & Pavot, W. (1993). Extroversion and neuroticism as predictors of objective life events: A longitudinal analysis. *Journal of Personality and Social Psychology, 65,* 1046–1053.

Martin, L., & Tesser, A. (1996). Some ruminative thoughts. In R. S. Wyer (Ed.), *Advances in social cognition* (Vol. 9, pp. 1–48). Hillsdale, NJ: Erlbaum.

Matthews, L. T., & Marwit, S. J. (2006). Meaning reconstruction in the context of religious coping: Rebuilding the shattered assumptive world. *Omega, 53,* 87–104.

McCrae, R. R., & Costa, P. T. (1986). Personality, coping, and coping effectiveness in an adult sample. *Journal of Personality, 54,* 385–404.

McCrae, R. R., & Costa, P. T. (1991). The NEO Personality Inventory: Using the Five-Factor Model in counseling. *Journal of Counseling and Development, 69,* 367–372.

McCullough, M. E., Pargament, K. I., & Thoresen, C. (2000). *Forgiveness: Theory, research, and practice.* New York, NY: Guilford Press.

McCullough, M. E., Root, L. M., & Cohen, A. D. (2006). Writing about the benefits of an interpersonal transgression facilitates forgiveness. *Journal of Consulting and Clinical Psychology, 74*, 887–897.

McGrath, J. C. (2006). Post-traumatic growth and the origins of early Christianity. *Mental Health, Religion & Culture, 9*, 291–306.

McGrath, J. C., & Linley, P. A. (2006). Post-traumatic growth in acquired brain injury: A preliminary small scale study. *Brain Injury, 20*, 767–773.

McIntosh, D. N., Silver, R. C., & Wortman, C. B. (1993). Religion's role in adjustment to a negative life event: Coping with the loss of a child. *Journal of Personality and Social Psychology, 65*, 812–821.

McMillen, J. C., & Fisher, R. H. (1998). The Perceived Benefits Scales: Measuring perceived positive life changes after negative events. *Social Work Research, 22*, 173–186.

Meraviglia, M. (2006). Effects of spirituality in breast cancer survivors. *Oncology Nursing Forum, 33*, E1–E7.

Morgan, D. L., Neal, M. B., & Carder, P. C. (1997). Both what and when: The effects of positive and negative aspects of relationships on depression during the first three years of widowhood. *Journal of Clinical Geropsychology, 3*, 73–91.

Mott, M. (1984). *The seven mountains of Thomas Merton.* Boston, MA: Houghton-Mifflin.

Murphy, P. E., Ciarrocchi, J. W., Piedmont, R. L., Cheston, S., Peyrot, M., & Fitchett, G. (2000). The relation of religious belief and practices, depression, and hopelessness in persons with clinical depression. *Journal of Consulting and Clinical Psychology, 68*, 1102–1106.

Neimeyer, R. A. (2000). Narrative disruptions in the construction of the self. In R. A. Neimeyer & J. D. Raskin (Eds.), *Constructions of disorder: Meaning-making frameworks for psychotherapy* (pp. 207–242). Washington, DC: American Psychological Association.

Neimeyer, R. A. (Ed.). (2001). *Meaning reconstruction and the experience of loss.* Washington, DC: American Psychological Association.

Neimeyer, R. A. (2006). Re-storying loss: Fostering growth in the posttraumatic narrative. In L. G. Calhoun and R. G. Tedeschi (Eds.), *Handbook of posttraumatic growth: Research and practice* (pp. 68–80). Mahwah, NJ: Erlbaum.

Neimeyer, R. A., Keesee, N. J., & Fortner, B. V. (2000). Loss and meaning reconstruction: Propositions and procedures. In R. Malkinson, S. Rubin, & E. Witztum (Eds.), *Traumatic and non-traumatic loss and bereavement* (pp. 197–230). Madison, CT: Psychosocial Press.

Neisser, U. (1994). *The remembering self: Construction and accuracy in the self-narrative.* New York, NY: Cambridge University Press.

Nightingale, V. R., Sher, T. G., & Hansen, N. B. (2010). The impact of receiving an HIV diagnosis and cognitive processing on psychological distress and posttraumatic growth. *Journal of Traumatic Stress, 23,* 452–460.

Oxman, T. E., Freeman, D. H., & Manheimer, E. D. (1995). Lack of social participation on religious strength and comfort as risk factors for death after cardiac surgery in the elderly. *Psychosomatic Medicine, 57,* 5–15.

Pargament, K. I., Desai, K. M., & McConnell, K. M. (2006). Spirituality: A pathway to posttraumatic growth or decline? In L. G. Calhoun & R. G. Tedeschi (Eds.), *Handbook of posttraumatic growth: Research & practice* (pp. 121–137). Mahwah, NJ: Erlbaum.

Pargament, K. I., Koenig, H. G., Tarakeshwar, N., & Hahn, J. (2004). Religious coping methods as predictors of psychological, physical, and spiritual outcomes among medically ill elderly patients: A two-year longitudinal study. *Journal of Health Psychology, 9,* 713–730.

Pargament, K. I., & Park, C. L. (1997). In times of stress: The religion-coping connection. In B. Spilka & D. McIntosh (Eds.), *The psychology of religion: Theoretical approaches* (pp. 43–53). Boulder, CO: Westview Press.

Pargament, K. I., Smith, B., Koenig, H. G., & Perez, L. (1998). Patterns of positive and negative religious coping with major life stressors. *Journal for the Scientific Study of Religion, 37*, 710–724.

Pargament, K. I., Tarakeshwar, N., Ellison, C. G., & Wulff, K. M. (2001). Religious coping among the religious: The relationships between religious coping and well-being in a sample of Presbyterian clergy, elders, and members. *Journal for the Social Scientific Study of Religion, 40*, 497–513.

Park, C. L. (2004). The notion of growth following stressful life experiences: Problems and prospects. *Psychological Inquiry, 15*, 69–76.

Park, C. L. (2005a). Religion as a meaning-making framework in coping with life stress. *Journal of Social Issues, 61*, 707–729.

Park, C. L. (2005b). Religion and meaning. In R. Paloutzian & C. L. Park (Eds.), *Handbook of psychology and religion* (pp. 295–313). New York, NY: Guilford Press.

Park, C. L. (2008). Testing the meaning-making model of coping with loss. *Journal of Social and Clinical Psychology, 27*, 970–994.

Park, C. L. (2009). Overview of theoretical perspectives. In C. L. Park, S. C. Lechner, & M. H. Antoni (Eds.), *Medical illness and positive life change: Can crisis lead to personal transformation?* (pp. 1–30.) Washington, DC: American Psychological Association.

Park, C. L., & Ai, A. L. (2006). Meaning-making and growth: New directions for research on survivors of trauma. *Journal of Loss and Trauma, 11*, 389–407.

Park, C. L., & Blumberg, C. J. (2002). Disclosing trauma through writing: Testing the meaning-making hypothesis. *Cognitive Therapy and Research, 26*, 597–616.

Park, C. L., Cohen, L. H., & Murch, R. (1996). Assessment and prediction of stress-related growth. *Journal of Personality, 64*, 71–105.

Park, C. L., Edmondson, D. E., Fenster, J. R., & Blank, T. O. (2008). Meaning-making and psychological adjustment following cancer: The mediating roles of growth, life meaning, and restored just-world beliefs. *Journal of Consulting and Clinical Psychology, 76,* 863–875.

Park, C. L., & Folkman, S. (1997). Meaning in the context of stress and coping. *General Review of Psychology, 1,* 115–144.

Park, C. L., Lechner, S. C., & Antoni, M. H. (Eds.). (2009). *Medical illness and positive life change: Can crisis lead to personal transformation?* Washington, DC: American Psychological Association.

Peterson, C. (2006). *A primer in positive psychology.* New York, NY: Oxford University Press.

Peterson, C., Park, N., Pole, N., D'Andrea, W., & Seligman, M. (2008). Strengths of character and posttraumatic growth. *Journal of Traumatic Stress, 21,* 214–217.

Phelps, L. F., Williams, R. M., Raichle, K. A., Turner, A. P., & Ehde, D. M. (2008). The importance of cognitive processing to adjustment in the first year following amputation. *Rehabilitation Psychology, 53,* 28–38.

Piedmont, R. L. (2004). Spiritual transcendence as a predictor of psychosocial outcome from an outpatient substance abuse program. *Psychology of Addiction Behaviors, 18,* 213–222.

Piedmont, R. L. (2005). The role of personality in understanding religious and spiritual constructs. In R. F. Paloutzian & C. L. Park (Eds.), *Handbook of the psychology of religion and spirituality* (pp. 253–273). New York, NY: Guilford Press.

Princeton Religion Research Center & Gallup Organization (1990's). Religion in America, Princeton, NJ: American Institute of Public Opinion.

Proffitt, D., Cann, A., Calhoun, L. G., & Tedeschi, R. G. (2007). Judeo-Christian clergy and personal crisis: Religion, posttraumatic growth, and well being. *Journal of Religion and Health, 46,* 219–231.

Ransom, S., Sheldon, K. M., & Jacobsen, P. B. (2008). Actual change and inaccurate recall contribute to posttraumatic growth following radiotherapy. *Journal of Consulting and Clinical Psychology, 76,* 811–819.

Resick, P. A., & Schnicke, M. K. (1992). Cognitive processing therapy for sexual assault victims. *Journal of Consulting and Clinical Psychology, 60,* 748–756.

Roberts, R. C. (2007). *Spiritual emotions: A psychology of Christian virtues.* Grand Rapids, MI: Eerdmans.

Rogers, C. (1959). A theory of therapy, personality and interpersonal relationships as developed in the client-centered framework. In S. Koch (Ed.), *Psychology: A study of science, volume three: Formulations of the person and social context* (pp. 184–256). New York, NY: McGraw-Hill.

Rogers, C. (1961). *On becoming a person.* Boston, MA: Houghton-Mifflin.

Rogers, C. (1964). Toward a modern approach to values: The valuing process in the mature person. *Journal of Abnormal and Social Psychology, 68,* 160–167.

Rosenberg, M. (1986). *Conceiving the self.* Malabar, FL: Krieger.

Salsman, J. M., Segerstrom, S. C., Brechting, E. H., Carlson, C. R., & Andrykowski, M. A. (2009). Posttraumatic growth and PTSD symptomatology among colorectal cancer survivors: A 3-month longitudinal examination of cognitive processing. *Psycho-Oncology, 18,* 30–41.

Schaefer, J. A., & Moos, R. H. (1992). Life crisis and personal growth. In B. N. Carpenter (Ed.), *Personal coping: Theory, research, and application* (pp. 149–170). Westport, CT: Praeger.

Schaefer, J. A., & Moos, R. H. (1998). The context of posttraumatic growth: Life crises, individual and social resources and coping. In R. G. Tedeschi, C. L. Park, & L. G. Calhoun (Eds.), *Posttraumatic growth: Positive changes in the aftermath of crisis* (pp. 99–125). Mahwah, NJ: Erlbaum.

Schroevers, M. J., Helgeson, V. S., Sandernnan, R., & Ranchor, A. V. (2010). Type of social support matters for prediction of posttraumatic growth among cancer survivors. *Psycho-Oncology, 19,* 46–53.

Schultz, J. M., Tallman, B. A., & Altmaier, E. M. (2010). Pathways to posttraumatic growth: The contributions of forgiveness and importance of religion and spirituality. *Psychology of Religion and Spirituality*, 2, 104–114.

Schulz, U., & Mohamed, N. E. (2004). Turning the tide: Benefit finding after cancer surgery. *Social Science & Medicine*, 59, 653–662.

Seligman, M. (2006). *Learned optimism: How to change your mind and your life*. New York, NY: Simon & Schuster.

Shahabi, L., Powell, L. H., Musick, M., Pargment, K. I., Thoreson, C. E., Williams, D., . . . Ory, M. A. (2002). Correlates of self-perceptions of spirituality in American adults. *Annals of Behavioral Medicine*, 24, 59–68.

Sheldon, K. M., & Lyubomirsky, S. (2006). How to increase and sustain positive emotion: The effects of expressing gratitude and visualizing best possible selves. *Journal of Positive Psychology*, 1, 73–82.

Sobel, A. A., Resick, P. A., & Rabalais, A. E. (2009). The effects of cognitive processing therapy on cognitions: Impact statement coding. *Journal of Traumatic Stress*, 24, 85–92.

Sommers-Flanagan, J., & Sommers-Flanagan, R. (2009). *Clinical interviewing*. Hoboken, NJ: Wiley.

Stanton, A., Bower, J. E., & Low, C. A. (2006). Posttraumatic growth after cancer. In L. G. Calhoun & R. G. Tedeschi (Eds.), *Handbook of posttraumatic growth: Research and practice* (pp. 138–175). Mahwah, NJ: Erlbaum.

Steger, M., & Frazier, P. (2005). Meaning in life: One link in the chain from religiousness to well-being. *Journal of Counseling Psychology*, 52, 574–582.

Stockton, H., Hunt, N., & Joseph, S. (2011). Cognitive processing, rumination, and posttraumatic growth. *Journal of Traumatic Stress*, 24, 85–92.

Sumalla, E., Ochoa, C., & Blanco, I. (2009). Posttraumatic growth in cancer: Reality or illusion? *Clinical Psychology Review, 29*, 24–33.

Taku, K., Cann, A., Tedeschi, R. G., & Calhoun, L. G. (2009). Intrusive versus deliberate rumination in posttraumatic growth across US and Japanese samples. *Anxiety, Stress & Coping, 22*, 129–136.

Taylor, R. D. (2010). Risk and resilience in low-income African American families: Moderating effects of kinship support. *Cultural Diversity and Ethnic Minority Psychology, 16*, 344–351.

Taylor, S. E. (1983). Adjustment to threatening events: A theory of cognitive adaptation. *American Psychologist, 38*, 1161–1173.

Tedeschi, R. G., & Calhoun, L. G. (1995). *Trauma and transformation: Growing in the aftermath of suffering*. Thousand Oaks, CA: Sage.

Tedeschi, R. G., & Calhoun, L. G. (1996). The Posttraumatic Growth Inventory: Measuring the legacy of trauma. *Journal of Traumatic Stress, 9*, 455–472.

Tedeschi, R. G., & Calhoun, L. G. (2004). Posttraumatic growth: Conceptual foundations and empirical evidence. *Psychological Inquiry, 15*, 1–15.

Tedeschi, R. G., & Calhoun, L. G. (2006). Expert companions: Posttraumatic growth in clinical practice. In L. G. Calhoun & R. G. Tedeschi (Eds.), *Handbook of posttraumatic growth: Research and practice* (pp. 291–310). Mahwah, NJ: Erlbaum.

Tedeschi, R. G., Park, C. L., & Calhoun, L. G. (1995). *Posttraumatic growth: Positive changes in the aftermath of crisis*. Mahwah, NJ: Erlbaum.

Tennen, H., & Affleck, G. (1998). Personality and transformation in the face of adversity. In R. G. Tedeschi, C. L. Park, & L. G. Calhoun (Eds.), *Posttraumatic growth: Positive changes in the aftermath of crisis* (pp. 65–98). Mahwah, NJ: Erlbaum.

Tomich, P., & Helgeson, V. (2006). Cognitive adaptation theory and breast cancer recurrence: Are there limits? *Journal of Consulting and Clinical Psychology, 74*, 980–987.

Tutu, D. (2004). *God has a dream: A vision of hope for our time.* New York, NY: Doubleday.

Updergaff, J. A., Silver, R. C., & Holman, E. A. (2008). Searching for and finding meaning in collective trauma: Results from a national longitudinal study of the 9/11 terrorist attacks. *Journal of Personality and Social Psychology, 95,* 709–722.

Unno, M. (2006). *Buddhism and psychotherapy across cultures: Essays.* Somerville, MA: Wisdom.

Van der Kolk, B. A. (2006). Clinical implications of neuroscience research in PTSD. *Annals of the New York Academy of Science, 1071,* 277–293.

Weaver, A. J., Flannelly, L. D., Garbarino, J. K., Figley, C. R., & Flannelly, K. J. (2003). A systematic review of research on religion and spirituality in the *Journal of Traumatic Stress*: 1990–1999. *Mental Health, Religion, & Culture, 6,* 215–228.

Weiss, T. (2002). Posttraumatic growth in women with breast cancer and their husbands: An intersubjective validation study. *Journal of Psychosocial Oncology, 20,* 65–80.

Weiss, T. (2004). Correlates of posttraumatic growth in husbands of breast cancer survivors. *Psycho-Oncology, 13,* 260–268.

Weiss, T., & Berger, R. (2010). *Posttraumatic growth and culturally competent practice: Lessons learned from around the globe.* Hoboken, NJ: Wiley.

Wicks, R. (2010). *Bounce: Living the resilent life.* New York, NY: Oxford University Press.

Wicks, R. (2012). *The inner life of the counselor.* Hoboken, NJ: Wiley.

Wiggins, J. S. (Ed.). (1996). *The Five-Factor Model of personality: Theoretical perspectives.* New York, NY: Guilford Press.

Wilson, J. T., & Boden, J. M. (2008). The effects of personality, social support, and religiosity on posttraumatic growth. *The Australasian Journal of Disaster and Trauma Studies, 1,* 1–19.

Wolchik, S. A., Coxe, S., Tein, J. Y., Sandler, I. N., & Ayers, T. S. (2008–2009). Six-year longitudinal predictors of posttraumatic growth in parentally bereaved adolescents and young adults. *Omega: Journal of Death and Dying, 58,* 107–128.

Wortman, C. B. (2004). Posttraumatic growth: Progress and problems. *Psychological Inquiry, 15,* 81–90.

Yalom, I. (1980). *Existential psychotherapy.* Yalom Family Trust.

Zoellner, T., & Maercker, A. (2006b). Posttraumatic growth in clinical psychology: A critical review and introduction of a two component model. *Clinical Psychology Review, 26,* 626–653.

Zoellner, T., Rabe, S., Karl, A., & Maercker, A. (2008). Posttraumatic growth in accident survivors: Openness and optimism as predictors of its constructive or illusory sides. *Journal of Clinical Psychology, 64,* 245–263.

SUBJECT INDEX

Author Index

Abraido-Lanza, A. F., 45, 103
Affleck, G., 6
Ai, A. L., 21, 57, 65, 73, 75, 167
Albert, S., 37
Alferi, S. M., 120, 123, 126, 139, 143
Allport, G. W., 173
Alonso, A., 120
Altmaier, E. M., 150, 151
American Psychiatric Association, 4
American Psychological Association (APA), 26
Andrykowski, M. A., 21, 46, 50, 104, 105, 121, 130, 133
Ano, A. G., 171, 172
Anonymous, 153, 157
Antoni, M. H., 12, 103, 104, 116, 119, 120, 123, 126, 138, 139, 140, 143
Aquinas, T., 164
Aspinwall, L. G., 119
Au, A., 169
Aviv, C., 169
Ayers, T. S., 49–50, 56

Bade, M. K., 169
Bandura, A., 121
Barton, J., 86, 87
Batson, C. D., 173
Baumeister, R. F., 57, 58, 74, 129

Bemporad, J., 159
Berger, R., 12, 140
Blanco, I., 35, 36, 38
Blank, T. O., 67, 73
Blumberg, C. J., 57, 62, 63
Boden, J. M., 116, 136, 174
Bower, J. E., 113, 119, 121
Bowlby, J., 129
Boy, A. V., 51
Boyers, A. E., 120, 123, 126, 139, 143
Boyraz, G., 103
Branigan, C., 97
Brazier, D., 180
Brechting, E. H., 46, 50, 104, 105
Brewin, C. R., 137
Brim, O. G., 97
Brockopp, D. Y., 121
Brown, G. W., 129
Butler, L., 18

Cadell, S., 21, 168
Calhoun, L. G., 7, 11, 12, 13, 14, 15, 17, 18, 21, 30, 32, 35, 44, 47, 52, 60, 65, 66, 68, 73, 77, 78, 79, 80, 81, 82, 85, 87, 88, 89, 90, 91, 92, 93, 95, 113, 116, 117, 119, 121, 122, 129, 131, 132, 134, 135, 137, 138, 140, 141, 143, 144, 160, 171, 173